The Art of Proofing

Preparing Your Dog For Obedience Trials

by

Adele Yunck

Photographs by Karen Taylor Photography

www.pawsinthegarden.com

and Adele Yunck

Illustrations by Kimberly Hundley

www.kimhundleyartist.com

and Adele Yunck

JABBY Productions
Ann Arbor, Michigan

The Art of Proofing:

Preparing Your Dog For Obedience Trials

by

Adele Yunck

Photographs by Karen Taylor and Adele Yunck

Illustrations by Kimberly Hundley and Adele Yunck

Published by: JABBY Productions
3676 W. Ellsworth Rd.
Ann Arbor, MI 48103

Copyright © 2008 by Adele Yunck

ISBN 978–0–9664574–1–4

All rights reserved. No part of this book may be reproduced or transmitted in any form or by any means, electronically or mechanically, including photocopying, recording, or by any information storage or retrieval system, except in the case of brief excerpts quoted in reviews, without written permission from the author or publisher.

First Edition, First Printing, 2008
Second Printing, 2014

Printed in the United States of America by
C-M Books, Inc., Ann Arbor, MI

To my beloved Treasure, my best girl.

This comes too late for you, but I will always be grateful for your inspiration and for always living up to your name.

Adele
2008

Table of Contents

Acknowledgements iv

General Proofing Concepts

1 Introduction..2

    Please Read This! 2

2 Why Do You Need Proofing?................................3

3 Terminology 5

4 My Training Philosophy 6

    Escape and Avoidance Training 7

    Types of Corrections 7

5 Be Prepared for Mistakes..................................9

    When your dog falls for the proof 9

6 Categories of Proofs......................................10

    Dogs..10

    People 10

    Noises and Noise Level................................. 11

    Footing 12

    Weather 13

    Time of Day..13

    Adjacent Activity 14

    Smells 14

    What You Will See In and Around the Ring........15

7 Progression of Proofs.....................................18

8 Timing of Proofs 20

9 Anticipation 21

10 Attention Proofing 22

Attention Loss 23

Distance Attention..23

Attention Game..24

Adding a Person Nearby 24

The 20 Treat Exercise 26

Solo Proofing of Attention 29

Group Attention Proofing Exercises 31

Empty the Toy Box...31

Moving Distracter 32

Applause 33

Noises 34

The Exercises

11 Heeling...36

12 Figure Eight 40

13 Sit and Down Stays 45

14 Fronts 53

15 Finishes 56

Automatic Finishes 58

16 Straight Recall and Drop on Recall 59

Basic Recall Distractions 59

UKC Drop on Recall...63

17 Novice Stand for Exam and the Utility Moving Stand.....65

Heeling into the Utility Stand...65

The Exam 66

The Moving Stand Call to Heel.......................................68

18 Retrieve on Flat 69

Retrieve Corrections for Errors Going to the Dumbbell.......69

Retrieve Proofs..69

Table of Contents ❖ iii

19 Retrieve over High Jump 78

20 Broad Jump 82

21 The Signal Exercise... 85

22 Scent Discrimination 95

23 Directed Retrieve... 100

24 Directed Jumping... 108

    Go-outs... 109

        Go-out Props... 109
        Taking the Go-out on the Road............................ 113
        General Go-out Tips.. 114
        Solutions to Common Go-out Errors...................... 114
        Food-Toss Sit 116
        General Go-out Proofs 117
        Proofing the Sit 117
        Proofing Against Stopping Short 119
        Proofing Against Taking a Jump on a Go-out.......... 120
        People Distractions... 120
        Gloves and Go-outs.. 120
            Stage 1—Go-outs with Decoy Glove 121
            Stage 2—Glove Retrieve Followed by Go-out 123
            Stage 3—Retrieve Followed by Go-out with
               Glove in Place 123
            Stage 4—Poison Bird...................................... 123

    Utility Jumping... 125

The End? 131

Appendix A: Truth is Stranger than Fiction 132

Appendix B: About the Author................................. 135

Appendix C: My Dogs & Their Titles........................ 137

Glossary 140

Index... 147

Acknowledgements

My thanks go to the many people who have attended my classes over the years, especially my weekly Proofing classes, as well as the many people who have taken private lessons. Loving novelty as I do, I enjoy dreaming up new, interesting, and sometimes downright devious tests for the dogs to conquer.

Thanks to my proofreaders. My father, **Robbins Burling**, once again offered his editing knowledge, greatly helping to clarify my meaning. **Jane Jackson** gave inordinately helpful suggestions on content and organization. **Marilyn Tomaszewski, Kathie Kryla,** and **Kathy Knol** were helpful with copy editing.

My deep gratitude to **Karen Taylor** (www.pawsinthegarden.com), whose photographic genius helped to bring my words to life.

Thanks to **Kim Hundley** (www.kimhundleyartist.com) for her illustrations, especially her patience while drawing the fabulous cover artwork.

Thanks to the handlers willing to be in the photographs:

| **Kay Braddock** and German Wirehaired Pointer **Jet** (U-CD Jed's Blue Angel CDX RE) | **Kay Braddock** and German Wirehaired Pointer **Hank** (Inverness Hammerin Hank RA) | **Colleen Heggarty** and Australian Terrier **Ole** (Ch Tatong's Paso Doble) |

❖ v

Bonnie Hornfisher and Nova Scotia Duck Tolling Retriever **Becky** (Becky CD RE OA AXJ)

Terry Jacobus and Shetland Sheepdog **Dakota** (Starfall's North by Northwest)

Joy Knapp and Beagle **Ranger** (U-CDX Echo Run Range Rover UD OA NAJ).

Jim Taylor and Golden Retriever **Fire** (Woodwalk Watch For Wildfire)

Belinda Venner and Labrador Retriever **Sparta** (U-AG1 Sparta Wolverine of Saline CDX RE OA OAJ CGC; RL3; CL2 CL3-R CL3-S CL4-S)

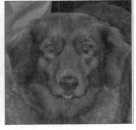

Corinne Williams and Nova Scotia Duck Tolling Retriever **Neon** (NS-DTRC/AKC/CKC/UKC CH U-CDX Lonetree's Neon Storm CDX RA OA OAJ JH WCI; Can CDX)

Adele's current dogs

Border Terrier
Joker (Kandu's
The Joker Is Wild
UD RE; RL2)

Flat-Coated Retriever **Sonic**
(Coastalight Primetime CD BN GN
RE SH WCX)

Finally, my deepest thanks to all of my dogs – Casey, Tramp, Rio, Treasure, Java, Joker, Gryffin, Ty, Sonic, and all the unknown future dogs – for the training you have given me. You have been the best teachers of all and I'm grateful for each of you.

General Proofing Concepts

1 Introduction

Even before Judy Byron and I initially published *Competition Obedience: A Balancing Act* in 1998, I wished for a small book that I could keep in my training bag. This book would contain oodles of ideas for proofing a dog for the obedience ring. Preparing a dog for the obedience ring is a long-term project, typically requiring several years for the advanced classes, and it isn't always simple to keep track of all the different distractions to which you should expose your dog or of those already mastered.

This is my attempt to provide such a book. It is not meant to be a complete, stand-alone training manual. My intent is to expand on the proofing ideas we recommended in *A Balancing Act*. I assume that the reader has an understanding of the overall structure of competition obedience, the individual exercises, and a general idea of what happens in an obedience trial. Judy and I covered that information in *A Balancing Act*, and there are several other books available on the subject.

While my overall philosophy has changed little in the twenty-plus years I've been training dogs, I have trained each of my own dogs a bit differently from the one before. I don't think any two dogs can be trained in exactly the same way. Don't be afraid to follow the training path that feels right to you. I have learned numerous useful tricks from or for each of my dogs to add to my training bag. I am also blessed with many wonderful students with fabulous dogs, and they've taught me a lot.

You will be spending far more time training your dog than you do actually showing him. Make the training time interesting, fun, and challenging. I hope that this book will help you to make this happen by sparking your own imagination.

Please Read This!

I encourage you to read the first part of this book (*General Proofing Concepts*) before diving into the individual exercises, since the early sections introduce many general ideas and provide a structure to use when you introduce your proofing.

2 Why Do You Need Proofing?

Proofing is a test. When you proof an exercise with your dog, you are testing his understanding of that exercise under increasingly difficult levels of distractions. Through proofing, you want to increase your dog's ability to ignore distractions and stay focused on you or the current exercise. When he does get distracted, you want him to get back on task promptly. If you do it properly, proofing builds confidence rather than eroding it.

Obedience trials are inherently distracting. Typically, they are held at unfamiliar places, often at fairgrounds with smells left over from the last county fair or family picnic. You and your dog are surrounded by strangers, some with clipboards, some with children in strollers, many with unfamiliar dogs, some with delectable smelling food.

> If you do it properly, proofing builds confidence rather than eroding it.

There may be loud speakers, hair dryers, clanging crates, and barking dogs. If you haven't exposed your dog to these smells, sights, and sounds before you enter him in an obedience trial, the chances are good that your dog will fail to perform as he does in familiar surroundings. In *Don't Shoot the Dog*, Karen Pryor calls this "the new tank syndrome." A dolphin, when moved to a new tank, needs time to acclimate to its new surroundings before being able to respond to cues in the same way it can in a familiar tank. Both you and your dog will need time and exposure to become habituated to the surroundings of a trial before both of you can perform well.

Taking the time with a puppy to do what dog people commonly call "socialization" will reduce the time needed later to prepare well for a trial. Socialization means taking your puppy on outings to new places and meeting new people without any expectations of good behavior. During these outings, you expose him to the equipment such as he'll see in his future obedience career, and an ample variety of sounds, places, machines, and people of all ages.

Your dog is not ready to show in a trial until you have proofed each exercise completely. What is completely? It depends in part on what you wish to accomplish with your dog. Would you be satisfied with any kind of passing score or do you strive for class placements? It also depends on what type of temperament your dog has. How aware is he of his environment? Is he a worrier, acting fearful, startling at any unusual or sudden noise? Is he nosy or exceedingly curious about what goes on around him? Both the worrier and the especially curious require more proofing than the average dog. Worrying too much can cause dogs to freeze up or come to a complete stop. Nosiness can distract dogs and lead them to forget their job.

Your proofing should be very easy at first, with you staying close to your dog, so that he will be more likely to succeed. While some errors are a natural consequence of proofing, you are trying to build your dog's confidence and have him succeed most of the time, not make him constantly fail.

> Start with easy proofing and increase the difficulty as your dog learns to succeed.

You should proof your dog to resist distractions in all situations: when stationary (stays and set-ups in heel position and front position); and when in motion—heeling, going away from you (retrieves, jumping, go-outs) and coming toward you (recalls, jumping, returning on retrieves).

3 Terminology

Before we go any further, I need to define several terms. *CR* refers to a conditioned reinforcer. Your CR is your way of marking what you like about what your dog has just done. It can be a click on a clicker, a special word or sound, or even a flash of light. It precedes a treat. When I say "CR" in the text, I mean, "use your CR and give your dog a treat."

When I use *distracter* in the text, it refers to another person who is helping you to proof your dog. *Distraction* usually refers to something inanimate, often an object your dog finds attractive, such as a squeaky toy or a tempting treat. It might also be a noise or smell of some kind.

I use the term *Phantom Food* to mean that your distracter holds her hand as if she is holding a treat out to your dog, usually with her fingers and thumb close together. She doesn't actually hold a treat during a Phantom Food proof.

Figure 3.1: I use Phantom Food as an early method of distracting dogs.

For simplicity's sake and following our convention in *Competition Obedience: A Balancing Act*, I use female pronouns for handlers and male pronouns for dogs. I hope neither men nor female dogs will take offense!

Within each exercise section, there are bulleted lists of proofing ideas. Some of these can be done by yourself. Some need one helper, and others require a group of people and often other dogs. The ways I use these different types of bullets are:

- For proofing by yourself, look for this single person bullet.
- For proofing with one helper, look for this two person bullet.
- For proofing with a group, often in a class setting, look for this group bullet.

4 My Training Philosophy

I start teaching by using *positive reinforcement*: I use my CR (conditioned reinforcer) to mark the desired behavior, and I give my dog something he desires (food, toy, attention from me, a game) immediately. I break an exercise into its smallest parts, and teach each individual part in isolation. After my dog understands that isolated part, I add corrections to it to decrease his response time and to increase the reliability of his response to the command. If you are going to use physical corrections, you will need to teach your dog how to respond as desired to a correction. When I use corrections, I want to see my dog make more effort, have sharper focus, and work with an improved attitude.

Next, I chain together parts, first in pairs, then in longer and longer chains until I have a complete exercise. When my dog understands each individual exercise required for a given class in a trial, I start to chain the exercises together into an entire routine, again starting with a pair of exercises, gradually adding to that chain.

It is essential that you precede any correction with a command. When I add a physical correction, I use a verbal correction ("ah, ah" said in a growly kind of voice) or a cue before the physical correction. This is so important! This cue can be either a verbal command or a hand signal. Silence in the trial ring should mean, "You are doing the right thing. Keep it up!" rather than "Look out, I may jerk your collar any time now!" Trainers often overlook this important point. By physically correcting your dog from silence, you teach him to mistrust silence. **The fair way is: verbal correction or cue, then physical correction**. This is fairer to your dog, and it builds more power into your verbal correction.

> Use a verbal correction or a cue *before* a physical correction.

When I add a correction, I want it first to be informative. I am telling my dog what he is doing wrong "in the moment." Any physical correction should be annoying or unpleasant enough that your dog wants to avoid it in the future. However, if you correct too strongly at first, your dog may decide to avoid you, too, so be careful how you add corrections. This is where "Know thy dog" is crucial.

General Proofing Concepts ❖ 7

Escape and Avoidance Training

The way in which I add corrections is called "escape and avoidance." This is the stage of training in which your dog learns that he must obey a given command or face the consequence—a correction. You are conditioning respect into the cue.

In the **escape** phase, you give a command and then a correction before your dog has a chance to respond. He should respond to escape any further correction. He learns that there is a choice he can make. This is *negative reinforcement*. I also call this an *automatic correction*. Do not correct if your dog responds immediately.

In subsequent situations, your dog **avoids** the correction altogether by responding promptly. It is extremely important to reinforce his efforts. From this training, your dog learns he has control over his actions and can predict and understand yours. This builds trust.

As a rule, you should not give food during the escape phase. Immediately after a correction, you should verbally praise your dog for the desired behavior, but the use of food should be a clear signal to him that his performance is correct or improved. Instead of feeding after a correction, immediately give your dog another chance to do it right without a correction. This effort earns a treat. If you start with the mildest correction, followed immediately by lots of praise, most dogs learn how to handle the correction and do not lose confidence.

Types of Corrections

You must temper physical corrections to fit your dog's temperament and size. When I started training my first dog, Casey, I had previously trained horses, so I was used to giving pretty strong jerks to my horse. I'm somewhat embarrassed to admit that I made little 12 lb. Casey fly through the air on several occasions because I didn't follow this basic training rule of tempering the correction to the size of the dog. I don't remember this being part of my early instruction. Fortunately, I did eventually figure it out all on my own.

Sometimes changing collars can make a difference in your dog's response to your corrections. A change from a buckle to a

My Training Philosophy

8 ❖ The Art of Proofing

pinch collar can make a radical improvement in your dog's response.

When using a correction that is intended to motivate your dog to action (a negative reinforcer), start with a mild correction, like a light tug on a buckle collar. Increase the level of correction as necessary until you find the right level for your dog. Don't get into "nagging," which means using frequent, insignificant corrections that don't change your dog's performance.

A correction serves as a *punisher* when it decreases a behavior. When using a correction as a punisher to eliminate a behavior, start with a strong correction.

You would want to use a negative reinforcer to improve your dog's response to your come command vs. a punisher to eliminate barking.

If your dog is not responding more frequently and correctly after you add a correction, the correction is not working as a reinforcer. If he is responding even less frequently than before you corrected him, it is serving as a punisher.

Praise should immediately follow your correction. This is extremely important! Do not make corrections in anger. Cultivate a playful attitude about corrections: "Whoops, I gotcha! Let's try again." If you find your dog quits after a correction, help him to obey the command—show him or physically guide him—or review the teaching steps.

A correction should motivate your dog to action, not shut him down. You should see a sharper focus, better attitude, and a decrease in response time when you incorporate corrections.

Too many people get in the bad habit of "babbling" to their dog—keeping up a constant flow of words at the dog, whether cue words or verbal praise. While this is helpful when first lengthening the time and distance your dog can work, he may come to depend on this. He must be weaned off extra talking before showing. Don't depend on your voice to get a ring performance from your dog!

> If your dog makes the same mistake twice in a row, change something—most likely simplify somehow—since he will almost undoubtedly make the same mistake a third time.

My Training Philosophy

5 Be Prepared for Mistakes

By its nature, proofing causes your dog to make mistakes. Before you start to proof an exercise, you need to have a plan in mind for what you are going to do when your dog falls for a distraction. This will help you react quickly to your dog's mistakes. Exactly how you react will depend on several factors:

- At what stage of training is your dog on this particular exercise? If you are just beginning to teach it, give the benefit of the doubt to your dog!

- How experienced is your dog overall? Inexperienced dogs will need more patience and a lighter hand.

- Is he confused by the proof? Don't correct if you think he is.

- Has he tried something, just not the right thing? Again, be patient, stop him from further error, and try again.

- Is he generally a bold and confident dog? Or does he so badly hate to be wrong that he gives up easily when he thinks he is wrong? With the latter type, you must be more careful in how you handle his errors. If you have a worrywart, start with very easy proofs.

Here is a basic plan of action to follow when your dog makes a mistake. Start with the first level and advance through the list until you find a successful level for your dog.

When your dog falls for the proof

1. **Try again.** Simply start the whole exercise over, or back up to just before the part on which your dog goofed or got sidetracked. Increasing the distance between your dog and the distraction often helps your dog succeed. After a few successes at the increased distance, decrease the distance and try the distraction again.

2. **Help your dog** complete the exercise despite the proof in whatever way works best with him, with verbal reminders or gentle physical guiding.

3. **Correct him verbally** at the instant of error, then try again.

4. **Correct him verbally and physically**, then try again.

6 Categories of Proofs

The novel environment of most obedience trial sites is overwhelming to the inadequately prepared dog. There are several variables to which you should gradually expose your dog in order to prepare him for competition. These include **other dogs; people**; **noises**, including their volume; the **footing** on which you show; **weather**; **time of day**; **surrounding activity**; **smells**; and the **sight picture** in and around the ring.

Dogs

Dogs are everywhere at obedience trials and dog shows. Some are beautifully trained, attending to their owner and ignoring everything else. Others have the barest minimum of training. These dogs are seen dragging their owners around the show grounds, visiting people and other dogs who don't necessarily want to be visited.

There will be many dogs moving around the grounds, going from inside to outside, from crate to ring and back. Some will be resting quietly in crates, while others who haven't learned to do so will be rattling about in their crate, sometimes whining and barking. There will be crate-protective rogues who scare passers-by with their sudden lunging and noise within the crate.

Many people get started in obedience training to train their dog to behave around other dogs and people. By attending obedience classes regularly, you give your dog a chance to learn to work sensibly around other dogs in a controlled setting. Early puppy socialization is a big help, too. Some dogs require a lot of time—counted in months, even years, not days—to settle down around other dogs. Sometimes patience on your part and maturity for your dog are the best antidotes.

Attending practice matches in a variety of places—if you have that luxury—is beneficial.

Many of the proofs I discuss throughout the book include using other dogs.

People

People are everywhere at a trial, both in the ring—the judge and ring stewards, and other exhibitors during group stays; and

General Proofing Concepts ❖ 11

out of the ring—other exhibitors, club members, vendors, and spectators. There may be crowds outside the ring you are working in, exhibitors and their dogs gathered in an adjacent ring during class awards, a crowd of Rally exhibitors walking a course in an adjacent ring, and parents pushing strollers, often with fussy or crying tots. If the kids aren't making noise, they are often eating something, typically at most dogs' nose level. Families sit right at ringside, sometimes eating hot dogs, popcorn, and ice cream. What would your dog do if a hot dog rolled into the ring near where he is working?

While some judges stay far across the ring from you during their judging, others move in very close, particularly during heeling, fronts and finishes. To best prepare your dog for this crowding, expose him to people with varying styles of dress, including flopping neck ties and necklaces, flapping skirts, hats, and rain clothes; different voices of varying volume; and diverse styles of movement, fast vs. slow, smooth vs. jerky.

In Novice and Open, you must heel your Figure 8's around and close to two ring stewards. Practice around people of different sizes, shapes, sexes, races, and ages, including children.

Noises and Noise Level

The noise level at trials can vary from the extreme quiet of some obedience trials, which makes any sound conspicuous, to the exhausting din of all-breed shows when they are held in big, echo-filled buildings. You need to consider and train for the types of noises you might encounter at an obedience trial or a dog show, including:

- Squeaky toys, since show photographers often use them during photo shoots. Some unkind handlers use them to warm up their dogs for the ring or as a reward after showing.

- Barking, whining, crying, or growling dogs.

- Hair dryers.

- Applause, often very sudden when a judge announces a winner or someone qualifies in Utility A.

- Talking and laughter.

Categories of Proofs

12 ❖ The Art of Proofing

- Dumbbells banging loudly on a wooden gymnasium floor, hitting walls, or crashing off the high jump when poorly thrown.

- Scent articles getting dumped onto the floor.

- A metal scent article getting dropped onto a metal chair.

- Banging of jump boards during jump height changes.

- Loudspeaker systems.

- Large fans.

- Rain on the roof.

- A thunderstorm.

- Crying babies.

- Crates being set up or taken down.

- Crate dollies rolling past with squeaking wheels. They can also contain barking dogs.

- Alarms.

- Traffic noises, including planes, cars, trains, and sirens.

- The general din of a dog show, with a lot of people, dogs, and activity in large, high-ceilinged rooms.

- Other trainers commanding their dogs too loudly or harshly.

- Banging or slamming doors.

- Popping bubble wrap. I encountered this at the National Obedience Invitational (NOI) in Tampa one year. We were showing in a ballroom where the carpet was covered in wide strips of plastic. It sounded like popping bubble wrap when people walked on it.

- High heels on stone floors, also encountered at the NOI. I've only run into this once, but it sure did distract my dog.

Footing

Obedience trials are held in a wide variety of venues, so it helps to learn what you are likely to encounter in your area of the country, so that you can be sure to adequately prepare your

Categories of Proofs

dog. I have seen trials held: inside on thin rubber or vinyl mats laid on concrete; inside on heavy rubber matting; inside on carpeting, especially at National Specialties; inside on dirt; inside on bare concrete; outside on grass; outside on dirt; under an outdoor pavilion, i.e. with open sides, with concrete and matting; under a tent with matting over a sloping asphalt parking lot (complete with potholes and resealed cracks underneath the matting). The tent had poles down the center.

You don't usually show on slippery linoleum floors, but you sometimes need to walk your dog across them to get to your ring, so you want him to be familiar with this type of flooring. You might need to walk on unfamiliar gravel. You may also need to go up or down a flight of stairs to reach your ring. If stairs are hard for you, an elevator ride may be required.

Dogs with thin skin and little hair, such as Min Pins and Whippets, typically dislike lying down on ridged mats, wet grass, or cold floors. Be sure to teach this early if you are training one of these breeds.

Weather

If you show outside, you need to be prepared for all kinds of weather, including blazing heat, high humidity, wind, rain, or freezing cold. While judges usually suspend judging at an outdoor trial if a thunderstorm is raging, the show usually continues at an indoor trial even when it's storming outside. There are many dogs who are so terrified by storms that they are unable to perform. Having experienced that with my first dog, I know how frustrating that can be.

Heat and cold can also pose problems. If, during the winter months, you train in a comfortably heated building, the cold floor of a drafty building may seem impossibly uncomfortable to a short-haired dog.

If you train in an air-conditioned building in the hot months and then show outside in the hot summer sun, many dogs, particularly those with black coats, will quickly melt if you haven't done at least some of your training outside.

Time of Day

You should consider the time of day you train your dog when you plan your training schedule. For the first four years that I

Categories of Proofs

showed my dogs, I worked during the day and did the bulk of my training in the evening, often after teaching obedience classes for a couple of hours first. My dogs were wired at 10 p.m., but since they were so used to sleeping during the day, it took considerable effort to get them up and working at daytime trials. I would suggest that you do as much of your training as you can at about the time of day you are likely to show. I realize that this isn't always practical, but do the best you can.

Adjacent Activity

You should train your dog to ignore any activity that can happen near your ring. You might be exhibiting in a ring next to another obedience ring with a dog running, jumping, retrieving, or a group stay; a conformation ring with running handlers and dogs, squeaky toys, and flying food; near agility, which includes a lot of running, leaping, and barking dogs, and a lot of loud bangs and whooshes as the dogs work on the equipment; near Rally, where handlers may talk a lot and may verbally correct their dogs, or a large group of handlers are walking a course; vendors, including those selling food; people sitting and having lunch or conversations at ringside; people running past with their dogs; doors opening or banging shut near your ring.

Smells

Smells will of course vary with the show site, but where there are people, there will probably be food vendors of some sort. If you are at a fairgrounds where people show livestock, there will be livestock smells for your dog to contend with. Remember how powerful a sense of smell your dog has.

Your dog may be distracted by smells that you don't even notice. After a couple of particularly dismal classes at a weekend's trials with my Border Terrier Java, I learned from Border Terrier-owning friends that the place had mice. It explained the excessive sniffing he did that weekend.

There will certainly be smells on the flooring in the ring. Exhibitors and judges walk on all kinds of surfaces and drag in smells on their shoes from outside the ring. An earlier dog may have had an accident, and the smell from the clean up solution will remain.

General Proofing Concepts ❖ 15

Finally, there are rude exhibitors who allow, or even encourage, their male dogs to pee on any available vertical surface, including ring gating or the stanchions that hold up the gates. This gives your dog yet another thing to distract him.

What You Will See In and Around the Ring

Indoor obedience rings are supposed to be fully matted. In my area of the country (the Midwest), most superintendents use 4–foot wide vinyl matting to cover the underlying floor. Sometimes these mats are taped together all along the seams. Small dogs are especially prone to noticing and avoiding tape, apparently viewing it as a barrier. I've seen small dogs jump taped seams, weave on heeling to avoid it, or stop at a strip of tape on a recall, sitting too far away to qualify. Many clubs have permanent 4–foot wide rubber matting installed in their buildings. This is the flooring I have in my training buildings.

I've shown at a trial in a pole barn whose end door was wide open during a gusting wind. While the Utility classes were going on, the mats along the side of the ring near the door were lifted up by the wind.

You need to consider the background behind you, particularly during Utility Signals. If your clothing blends in with the background too much, your dog may have trouble seeing your signals. If you are backlit because of glare from a window or a suddenly opened door, you may appear as nothing but a silhouette to your dog.

Flies and bugs are a terrible irritant to many dogs. Since they aren't exactly predictable, there's no simple way to train for them, but judicious use of your CR and treats when flies are around should help to reduce his irritation. Tickling him with a dangling object on a string may help to simulate landing flies.

In spite of a trial committee's best efforts to provide clean rings, a great variety of things can find their way to the floor in or just outside the ring, such as:

- Scraps of paper.

- Food.

- Toys.

Categories of Proofs

16 ❖ The Art of Proofing

- Hair balls, especially tumbleweed ones blowing across the floor when you show near a grooming area.

- Grass clippings or bits of straw.

- Holes in the matting.

- Sunlight patches from nearby windows.

- Floor grates or drains under matting that clank when someone steps on them.

- Colored sticky dots, chalk marks, or smiley faces, which judges use to mark their ring, such as where the stewards stand for the Figure 8's or where you need to set up for an exercise.

When you show outside, the ground is likely to be uneven, and a recent rainstorm may leave puddles. You might encounter long, wet grass. I showed in obedience at a particularly memorable National Specialty with such long grass that I had to practically wade through it during heeling. It did not make for the smoothest of handling.

Rings are enclosed in a variety of ways, often dependent on where you show. In my area, rings are usually surrounded by baby gates held up by colored stanchions (Figure 6.1). I've also seen rings surrounded by curtains tall enough to prevent most dogs from seeing over. You might see a ring with posts connected with chains (Figures 6.2). To a short dog, rings defined by stakes and ropes, chains, or plastic flagging don't even appear to have a barrier. The barrier that you look down on is far above the short dog's head.

Categories of Proofs

General Proofing Concepts ❖ 17

Figure 6.1: This Rally ring is surrounded by baby gates and stanchions. Note the masking tape covering all the seams in the mats. Some dogs will avoid tape used this way.

Figure 6.2: This conformation ring is surrounded by posts and chains, which are above a short dog's head.

Progression of Proofs

7 Progression of Proofs

I strongly recommend that you start taking your dog to novel locations early in his training and as often as possible. Many people do all of their teaching, training, and proofing in the same one or two locations and then are surprised when their dog cannot work at a trial in an unfamiliar place.

If your dog is easily startled or frightened, you should proof more slowly and carefully than if your dog is bold and confident. It is essential for you to take the "scaredy-cat" dog to a variety of places without expecting much from him. Let him learn to relax in new places before you put training demands on him.

I look at training and proofing as a staircase (Figure 7.1). Each step leading up represents a stage in your dog's understanding of an exercise. When you first start training your dog to do a new exercise, you are at the bottom of the staircase. When you walk in a ring at a trial, you should be at or very near the top of the staircase for each exercise required for that particular class level. At the very least, you should be a few steps above the one with "dog demonstrates understanding" on it. When you go to a novel place to train or add in a distraction in a familiar place, you should move back down a step or two in what you expect from your dog. If an exercise really falls apart, you might even have to return briefly to the bottom of the staircase before starting up

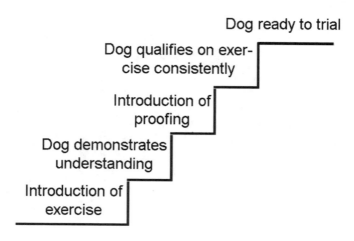

Figure 7.1: The training and proofing staircase.

General Proofing Concepts ❖ 19

again. Extract the hard part, whatever it happens to be, from the whole exercise, and focus only on that part. Don't be afraid of this process! Typically, **proofing exposes weaknesses in the foundation training you've given your dog.** In part, that is what proofing is supposed to do for you: expose any weaknesses.

Though I will ultimately need to stand across the ring from my dog—35–45 feet away—on many exercises, it is still important to start out close by. Because I am nearby, I can help my dog respond properly, and add a correction if I need to. When a distraction causes him to goof even with me close by, he certainly will not be able to respond correctly when I am 45 feet away, as he will be during many exercises, such as recalls or Directed Jumping.

When you introduce a new proof to your dog, stay closer to him than you would when training somewhere familiar or when nothing else is going on. Let's assume your dog responds consistently to your drop command during the Drop on Recall exercise when he starts 40 feet from you and you cue him to drop when he is about 20 feet away. You decide to add a friend standing alongside your dog's recall path. Move down the distance staircase and start 10 feet closer to your dog—30 feet away. Cue him to drop when he is 15 feet from you.

> Each time you introduce a new proof, decrease the distance between you and your dog.

Many people enter their dogs in obedience trials with inadequate proofing. This results in their dog failing one or more exercises. It's better to find out in training what your dog really understands about an exercise. It's also a lot less expensive than wasting the cost of an entry fee.

Progression of Proofs

20 ❖ The Art of Proofing

8 Timing of Proofs

Distractions can happen at any time you are in the ring. They can happen before you start an exercise and they can happen during any part of an exercise. To be complete about your proofing, you should practice with distractions just before you start an exercise and during all of its many parts.

Introduce the following distractions before you cue your dog. When you first introduce a given distraction, you might, if necessary, delay your cue briefly to allow your dog's attention to return to you. As your dog gains experience, your cue should immediately follow the distraction. When that is successful, the distraction should happen right after your cue.

It is best if you have a friend who can do the following proofs for you, but you can work many of these by yourself, too. I recommend you advance through these from top to bottom.

- Squeak a toy.
- Crinkle a treat bag.
- Drop a toy.
- Drop a treat bag.
- Drop a dumbbell.
- Throw a toy.
- Throw a dumbbell.
- Throw a treat bag.

Timing of Proofs

9 Anticipation

Anticipation means your dog does an exercise or part of an exercise without you cueing him with your usual verbal command or hand signal. Since there are many exercises in which you NQ (non-qualify) if your dog anticipates some part of it, proofing against anticipation is an important part of training. Anticipation is a common learning stage and often simply means that you haven't reinforced the previous part of the exercise often enough.

Many dogs who are shown regularly learn the judge's commands and obey the judge instead of waiting for their handler. Some commonly anticipated commands are "Finish," "Fast," and "Forward." Anticipation of "Stand your dog!" on the *Moving Stand* exercise is also a prevalent problem.

Have a friend repeat the anticipated command several times. You should be poised to interrupt your dog if he responds to her commands instead of waiting for yours. You can also reinforce your dog—CR, treat, and release—when he ignores your friend's commands.

For example, if your dog comes before you call him on a recall, you need to add distractions to the stay and reinforce him more often for resisting the stay distractions. You might have a friend play judge and say "Call your dog!" loudly while gesturing enthusiastically with her arm. When your dog starts to come before you call him, immediately use a verbal correction and move toward him. Take him back to the spot where you left him and start over. When your dog resists this and stays in place, praise from across the room and sometimes walk back to give a treat, a toy, or possibly release. When your dog resists this level of distraction, add having your friend moving around behind your dog while issuing the command and waving her arm.

You should know the regulations well enough that you know when anticipation is an NQ vs. a simple point deduction.

10 Attention Proofing

Attention is one of the cornerstones of solid obedience work. Whenever your dog sits in heel position as you start an exercise (Figure 10.1), it is important for him to be focused on you. Any time he returns, as in a recall (Figure 10.2), he needs to pay attention to your position in order to do his sit in front properly, as well as being ready to finish. It is usually easier for new trainers to start training stationary attention rather than moving attention, so this is the step on which I introduce distractions.

Figure 10.1: Java is sitting in heel position, watching me. He was only 6 months old when this was taken.

Attention often means that your dog is looking at you, but he also needs to stay focused on the entire exercise. If he runs out to his dumbbell during a retrieve and then stands over it, staring at something outside of the ring, you have lost his attention.

Figure 10.2: This shows front position attention. Note the dog's head position, with his nose high, centered on his handler's body.

If you are fortunate to have a dog with natural attention, your training life will be vastly simpler. Most dogs who ignore their handlers have not been taught the importance of paying attention to their handler while ignoring the environment. *Competition Obedience: A Balancing Act* contains a full description of how I teach attention, but, to summarize here, I start by using my CR (conditioned reinforcer) and giving a treat anytime my puppy or dog glances at me, gradually working for longer and longer periods of focused attention in formal positions. Once my dog can remain focused on me for at least 5 seconds, I add a verbal and a physical correction when he loses attention.

Attention Loss

What should you do when your dog looks at a distraction? It depends on where he is on the attention-training staircase. Review the *My Training Philosophy* (pp. 6-8) and *Be Prepared for Mistakes* (p. 9) sections.

When my dog is in heel position and he looks away instead of focusing on me, the physical corrections I use, in approximate order of mildest to strongest, are:

- Tap on the head.

- Leash pop up on a buckle collar.

- Leash pop up on a prong collar.

- Bump with my left knee.

- Shoulder tag or tweak with a release after.

- Bonk on the head.

- Grab neck hair or skin and tweak.

I precede any one of these physical corrections with a verbal correction or cue.

Distance Attention

There are several situations when your dog should watch you from a distance. By the time you are in Utility, your dog must be able to keep his attention on you when he is in:

A sit:

- While you walk away on the Novice and Open recalls.

- When you leave him for the Open *Broad Jump*.

- After the sit on the Utility *Signal Exercise*.

- After he sits on the go-out portion of *Directed Jumping*.

A down:

- After the drop on the *Drop on Recall.*
- After the drop on the *Signal Exercise.*

A stand:

- During the Novice *Stand for Exam.*
- After the Utility *Signal Exercise* stand stay.
- Throughout the Utility *Moving Stand for Exam.*

Attention Game

A useful game to foster distance attention is to combine it with either food-toss or toy retrieve games. Toss your treat or toy a few times and have your dog retrieve it. Then, if you are using a toy, fake a throw and call for a sit once he's run out a short distance from you. If you are using food, call for a sit just after he eats his treat. Once he is in a sit, wait for him to focus his attention on you, CR, then release with another toy or food throw off behind him or to the side. This helps reduce creeping toward you. As soon as your dog can do position changes (down to sit, stand to down, etc.) at a distance, you can start requiring one or more before the next release to a toy or a treat.

Adding a Person Nearby

If, during any of these distractions, your dog "loses it," by which I mean he becomes so drawn to the distraction that he cannot hold his heel position sit, have your distracter move farther away from you.

Set up with your dog sitting in heel position. Start with a distracter simply standing nearby. Nearby for a more focused dog could be 4 feet away, while for a highly social one, it might be 20 feet away. Remember to use your CR and give a treat to your dog when he stays focused on you. Once your dog can remain focused on you with the distracter standing still in various places around you—in front, to either side, behind you—start to progress through the following list:

- 👥 Distracter bends over.
- 👥 Distracter bends over and pats her legs.
- 👥 Distracter bends over, pats her legs, and sweet talks your dog.
- 👥 Distracter moves in an arc back and forth in front of you, from one side to the other. She should be "nearby" for your dog, whatever that distance is. She should gradually turn the arc into a circle with you and your dog in the center of the circle. On successive circles, she should get closer and closer until she is within two feet of you and your dog. This might take one training session. It might take much longer. It depends how social your dog is.
- 👥 Distracter bends over and:
    - Extends her hand, with Phantom Food, i.e., she pretends to hold food in her fingertips but doesn't really (Figure 10.3).
    - Offers real food.

Figure 10.3: I am holding out *Phantom Food*, which most dogs think is actually food. If a dog is too interested, I open my hand to show him there's nothing there.

Attention Proofing

26 ❖ The Art of Proofing

- • Offers a toy.

- • Waves a toy.

👥 Distracter drops a soft toy.

👥 Distracter squeaks a toy.

👥 Distracter crinkles a bag of treats.

👥 Distracter tosses a soft toy.

👥 Distracter squeaks and then tosses a toy.

👥 Distracter pets your dog (Figure 10.4).

👥 Distracter squats down and repeats the previous series.

👥 Distracter carries helium balloons or ties them to her waist. If your dog has never seen balloons, give him a chance to investigate them. Some dogs are quite frightened of them at first.

The 20 Treat Exercise

You can start this exercise as soon as your puppy knows that voluntary attention is a Good Thing. Voluntary attention means that when your dog spontaneously looks at you without a command, you tell him he's right by using your CR and giving a treat.

While there is nothing particularly magical about the number 20 in this exercise, I recommend it as a starting point for the number of repetitions you should do. Of course you may vary this number to suit your dog.

Start with 20 treats that are the same size as the treats you usually use. You will also need a stopwatch or at least a watch with a second hand.

To train this exercise, take your dog to a novel location, ideally one that is not terribly distracting when you first start. Have your treats ready before you get your dog out of your car, so that you don't broadcast to him that you are carrying food. Let him sniff around for a few minutes and relieve himself if needed, but don't wait too long. Then start your stopwatch.

Every time your dog looks at you, CR and treat, then resume being quiet. Keep watching your dog but keep quiet. With a beginning dog, I don't expect him to be in any particular position in

Attention Proofing

General Proofing Concepts ❖ 27

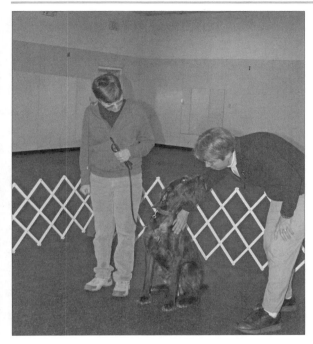

Figure 10.4: I am petting Hank while he sits in heel position. In the top photo, he is very distracted. In the bottom one, he is ignoring me and watching Kay.

Attention Proofing

28 ❖ The Art of Proofing

relation to me, but as he gains experience, I typically have my dog sitting in heel position or front position.

You want to learn two things:

How long does it take your dog to look at you voluntarily the first time?

How long does it take him to look 20 times?

Write both of these numbers down somewhere, along with where you trained the exercise. A calendar is a good place to record the data, because it will remind you of how long it has been since you last trained the exercise. If you do it often enough, you should see these numbers shrink.

What do these numbers mean? If the first one is lengthy—I've had students report 20 minutes—it tells you a couple of things. First, if you have not had your dog out in novel places much, it shows you that you will need patience while he learns to resist distractions and focus on you. This is important for you to learn so you can plan your training program. Second, if he still takes a long time in spite of experience, it tells you that your dog needs a lot of time to settle in, or to get *habituated*, at a new place before he himself can bring his attention to you.

If it takes your dog a long time to look at you 20 times, it probably means he has a short attention span, and you would be smart to work this exercise frequently to build his attention stamina. It might help to do this first in an area where the distractions are less stimulating. Your front yard with the neighbor's cat wandering around is typically too advanced for beginning dogs.

Finally, if your dog needs only a short time to look at you 20 times, it usually means that you have a food-driven dog—once your dog figures out that you have food, he rivets his attention on you, and you go through your 20 treats rapidly.

What do you do if, after the first treat, your dog stares at you? Bless your dog, and reinforce? Absolutely! But kidding aside, move around the training area to allow him to get distracted again. If this still doesn't take up much time, you can also start waiting for longer-duration attention, rather than simply reinforcing the instant he glances at you. You can also train the exercise in a busier place.

Attention Proofing

General Proofing Concepts ❖ 29

I have found this 20 treat voluntary attention exercise to be a great way to kick start a somewhat more experienced dog's training session in a busy place. I do this voluntary attention exercise until my dog is more focused on me than his surroundings. Then I start demanding more work from him. While I eventually use corrections for loss of or lack of attention, I have found that a dog who learns voluntary attention focuses his attention on his handler in quite a different way than one who has been corrected into paying attention. The voluntarily attentive dog tends to be more relaxed and confident, with "Ears up, eyes bright," as Patty Ruzzo used to say. The dog who is corrected into paying attention tends to act stressed, licking his lips, yawning, darting his eyes around, and with his ears laid back.

Solo Proofing of Attention

There are many different ways in which you can distract your dog when you are training alone:

- With your dog in heel position, drop something from your right hand, such as hard treats that will make a noise and draw your dog's attention toward the floor. Styrofoam packing peanuts flutter slowly to the floor, providing a visual distraction.

- Drop or toss a toy in increasingly tempting ways, and when your dog refocuses or stays focused on you, you can release him to the toy.

  - Drop it at your side without any fanfare.

  - Toss it slightly out to the side.

  - Toss it slightly out in front of you.

  - Toss it over your head so it drops on the floor to your dog's left.

- Use a TV remote control to turn your TV on or to change channels.

- Open your refrigerator door.

- Make noise with your feet, tapping your toes or scuffing your foot along the floor.

- Squeak a toy with your foot.

- Nudge a ball with your foot, causing it to roll away slowly.

Attention Proofing

- Toss a ball off to your right, gently at first, gradually tossing more energetically so that it bounces. Vary the direction in which you throw it.

- Work in front of stores with automatic doors and passing pedestrians.

- Attach helium balloons to your waist, then eventually to your dog's collar. This is especially helpful for the dog who tends to notice things that hang from the ceiling. Do this with caution—you don't want to petrify your dog. Start with the balloons tied to a chair or a baby gate if you need to.

- Hang a toy on a baby gate and work nearby, whether heeling, recalls, or retrieves (Figure 10.5). Also note the sticky dot on the floor in the picture. Many dogs are attracted to dots, which some judges use to mark the floor for various reasons.

Figure 10.5: Hang a toy from a baby gate and work nearby. Note the light-colored sticky dot on the floor. They are remarkable dog-nose magnets, drawing dogs to sniff them.

Group Attention Proofing Exercises

The following sections explain some of the proofing exercises I use in my group classes. The distracter mentioned is usually me, the instructor. If you are training with a group of friends, take turns acting as distracter.

Empty the Toy Box

I usually start this exercise in my second 6-week competition obedience class.

All members of the group start with their dogs sitting in heel position along one side of the training floor, facing the distracter (Figure 10.6). The distracter is at the other side of the area with a box or bag with a variety of toys, especially squeaky ones, dumbbells, gloves, and other noisemakers. The goal for each person is to approach as close to the distracter as possible. The distracter stays in one place making a racket or distracting motion with each item from her box, squeaking the squeaky toys, dropping dumbbells, tossing gloves or soft toys high in the air, etc. When your dog successfully keeps his focus on you through two noises or tosses in a row, take two giant steps towards the distractions.

Figure 10.6: These handlers are ready to start the "empty the toy box" exercise. Note that all of the dogs are watching their handlers.

Attention Proofing

32 ❖ The Art of Proofing

Figure 10.7: The handlers whose dogs are watching well have moved closer to the distractions during the "empty the toy box" exercise. The dogs near the back are having trouble staying focused on their handlers, so their handlers are staying at the starting location.

Each person can move closer as rapidly as her dog is ready, while those with less-attentive dogs stay as far away as needed for success (Figure 10.7).

Many dogs, when first confronted with a squeaking toy, turn their full attention to that and away from their handler. When I use a squeaky toy in a class, I keep squeaking rhythmically. Most dogs eventually tire of it and suddenly remember they have a teammate and bring their attention back to their handler.

Early in my dog's training, I prefer to wait for him to refocus on me rather than correcting him into watching me. As he gets more advanced, I do correct him when he looks away, using a verbal correction followed by a leash pop.

Moving Distracter

All members of the group gather in a circle facing in, with their dogs sitting in heel position, with 8–10 feet between dogs. The distracter walks around the dogs in various ways:

- 👥 On the inside of the circle clockwise and counterclockwise.

Attention Proofing

General Proofing Concepts ❖ 33

- On the outside of the circle clockwise and counterclockwise, first walking and later running. I sometimes holler "Let's go get a cookie!" as I run.
- Weaving around between the handlers.
- Circling each dog and handler clockwise.
- Circling each dog and handler counterclockwise.
- As the dogs gain experience, add a dog heeling with the distracter to each of the above proofs (Figure 10.8).

When the dogs succeed with each proof listed, the handlers step toward the center of the circle, so they are closer to the dogs and handlers on each side, and repeat the whole process.

Applause

Half the group works on stationary attention while the other half applauds in the following ways:

- Polite, relatively quiet applause, like that given at the end of a class during the class awards, when the judge asks everyone to thank the ring stewards.

Figure 10.8: Terry, Colleen, and Belinda are working on stationary attention while Joy and Ranger work on moving attention.

Attention Proofing

34 ❖ The Art of Proofing

♦♦♦ More enthusiastic and louder applause.

♦♦♦ Add an occasional "whoop" to the applause.

♦♦♦ The type of applause when someone finishes their UD
title—rowdy and raucous!

You should use applause to proof all of the obedience exercises, since there can be applause any time you are in the ring.

Noises

The section on *Noises and Noise Level* (pp. 11-12) lists the sounds to which I suggest you expose your dog. You will probably think of others to add to the list. Start with the sound far enough away from your dog so that he has a reasonable chance to succeed in keeping his attention on you. When the current step is mastered, move the noise closer to your dog, or your dog closer to the noise. If possible, I suggest that you present each noise:

- Before your command.

- After your command.

- With a combination of movement and noises by the distracter.

The Exercises

11 Heeling

My ideal picture of a smooth heeling team is similar to a dance team. When the judge gives an order, the handler responds promptly but not abruptly. She gives consistently clear but subtle cues to her dog, who trots smoothly and attentively at her left side, the team moving with precision through turns, pace changes, and halts.

I contend that after you thoroughly teach your dog how to heel—teaching attention first, then all of the individual parts of heeling before combining them in any way—then most points lost during heeling exercises in an obedience trial happen because of attention errors. Your dog might startle at a door slam or a dumbbell landing in the next ring. Even such a very brief loss of focus can cause a small position error. It can also cause a blunder like failing to sit when you stop. While I strive for 100% attention from my dogs, especially during heeling, I also train them to refocus promptly when they do lose focus. Proofing helps this.

Proofing of heeling is primarily proofing attention while in motion. Refer back to the *Categories of Proofs* (pp. 10-17) and *Attention Proofing* (pp. 22-34) sections and use those ideas to proof your heeling. Expose your dog to the various proofs while you work on the different elements of heeling, such as halts, turns, and pace changes. Remember, proofing reveals weaknesses in your dog's understanding of an exercise or part of an exercise. When you discover a weakness, isolate that piece and train it separately from the whole exercise. Strengthen it and then reinsert it into the exercise. See *Attention Proofing* (pp. 22-34) for how I handle attention loss and review the *Be Prepared for Mistakes* (p. 9) section.

These are some of the most important proofs to do while you heel with your dog:

- Have a friend walk along with you, either behind you, in front of you, or to either side. This simulates heeling in the ring with a judge nearby. Sometimes have her carry a clipboard. Many dogs are bothered when a stranger walks nearby like judges do while judging. (Figures 11.1 and 11.2).

The Exercises ❖ 37

Figure 11.1: Many dogs are bothered when a stranger walks nearby like judges do while judging heeling. In this photo, Hank made a substantial error on the halt because of how closely I was following him.

Figure 11.2: With me a bit farther away, Hank did an excellent halt. This is something Kay needed to do a lot with Hank to get him comfortable with someone in his space.

Heeling

38 ❖ The Art of Proofing

- 👥 Have a friend make a sudden noise during about turns and halts, such as slamming a door or dropping a dumbbell.

- 👥 Have a friend cause distractions at the end of the ring where you do about turns.

- 👥 Have someone call heeling patterns for you; *lots* of patterns.

- 👥👥 Set up a set of four baby gates. You can use these in several ways. A few possibilities:

  - Have four people heeling together, each using one of the four quadrants (Figure 11.3).

  - Have four people doing a series of right or left turns with a turn into the next quadrant after each turn. If timed right, there will be several dogs heeling into the corners at the same time (Figure 11.4).

  - Have some dogs doing sit or down stays in one quadrant while others are heeling nearby.

- 👤 Heel right up to a baby gate. Practice halts and any of the turns right next to one.

Figure 11.3: These four baby gates are set up to create four separated areas. This can be used for all sorts of proofing combinations of many different exercises. In a class setting, four people can heel in various ways in each area.

Heeling

Figure 11.4: These teams are heeling from one quadrant to the next, making a left U-turn around the end of the gating.

- Have someone wiggle a baby gate while you heel nearby, as unsupervised children might do at a trial.

- Place a toy on the floor and heel nearby. When I started doing this with Gryffin, "nearby" was 60 feet away from the toy! Start with a moderately interesting toy, advancing to a favorite. On the day Gryff earned the 3rd leg of his CD, I was very glad I had worked this proofing so much with him. While we were warming up for our turn, he saw one of the stewards putting the toy prizes out on a table just outside the ring. The steward (fortunately) changed her mind and put them back in the box, but Gryffin remembered. Twice during the heeling, when we were near the end of the ring by the table, he did a quick peek to see if they were there. My back was to the table on the recall and he came barreling at me. When I released him after his finish, instead of moving forward as he usually did, he zipped behind me as though to say "Do I get one of these toys NOW?" I'm sure that if I hadn't trained him so often with toys on the floor, he would have deserted me to run to the table.

Heeling

12 Figure Eight

The Figure Eight exercise begins from a starting point equidistant between two people who serve as posts. The posts stand eight feet apart and the handler faces the judge, with the dog sitting in heel position. I like to start approximately three feet back from the imaginary line connecting the posts. The dog and handler walk briskly around the two posts two complete times, making two Figure Eight's. The judge will call at least two halts during this exercise: at least one during the exercise and one at the end. The Figure Eight in the Novice class is done on-leash; the one in Open is off-leash. The handler may go in either direction and there are no pace changes in the Figure Eight. When training Figure 8's, you can do any of the proofs you do during heeling. Here are some additional ideas to work on during Figure 8's:

- For those handlers who start their Figure 8's to the left, the transition line from the left arc to the right arc (C–A–D in Figure 12.1) is one of the most critical parts of the whole exercise. If your dog doesn't accelerate enough before the right arc, he will lag as you go around the right post. Because it is so important, be sure to spend ade-

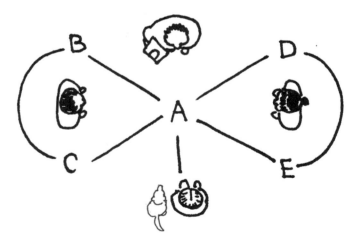

Figure 12.1: The line C–A–D is the critical place for the dog to accelerate to arc around the right post.

quate time proofing your dog's attention as you move through this part of the exercise.

- When you train alone and have to use inanimate posts, hang a coat and hat from your posts (Figure 12.2). A feather duster makes an exotic post topper.
- Have the people acting as Figure 8 posts:
  - Wiggle their fingers.
  - Pat their legs.
  - Offer Phantom Food.
  - Offer real food.
  - Cough, sneeze, or sniff.
  - Squeak a toy.
  - Turn circles in place.
  - Tap their feet.
  - Do jumping jacks.

Figure 12.2: Joker was distracted by the bait bag hanging from the coat pocket at first.

Figure Eight

- For an advanced dog, have the posts play a game of catch with a soft toy.
- Some judges move quite a bit during the Figure 8 exercise, in order to see the team from all sides, so be sure to prepare your dog for this possibility.
- Use large stuffed toys on the floor or in a chair as your posts.
- Have a distracter positioned as shown in Figures 12.3–Figure 12.5. She can do any of the now familiar distractions: bend over, squat, drop something, etc.
- Train with people posts of different sizes, shapes, sexes, races, and ages.
- Use a couple of food bowls as distractions—like the Offset Figure 8 from Rally Obedience—each placed about 3 feet from the center point, where you normally start your Figure 8 and where most judges initially stand. In Rally, the bowls are supposed to be covered, while still allowing any odors from smelly treats to escape. Instead, a toy might be sitting in the bowl. If your dog is too distracted with the bowls this close, start with them farther away, gradually moving them closer and closer to the path you heel with your dog.

Figure 12.3: I am positioned at a critical place on the Figure 8, ready to try to distract Ranger.

Figure Eight

The Exercises ❖ 43

Figure 12.4: Ranger fell for the distraction—a big hunk of treat—the first time I waved it nearby.

Figure 12.5: Ranger resists the big treat his next time around.

Figure Eight

44 ❖ The Art of Proofing

- 👤 Use the loaded Rally food bowls as your posts.

- 👥 Have a trustworthy dog do a sit stay and serve as a post with his handler standing 8 feet away serving as the 2nd post. This proofs not only your dog's attention, but the stay of the dog serving as post.

- 👤 Use bar jump uprights for your posts and hang singing or noise-making toys from the pins that normally hold up the bar. The height at which you hang the toys can be adjusted to the size of your dog.

- 👥👥 Have a group of handlers with trustworthy dogs act as posts, alternating dogs and handlers (Figure 12.6). Have the dogs and handlers positioned 8 feet apart in all directions. This proofs not only your dog's attention, but the stays of the dogs serving as posts. Do be careful of the post dogs' tails.

Figure 12.6: Joy and Ranger are working on Figure 8's around many trustworthy dog and handler teams, who are set up 8 feet apart in each direction.

Figure Eight

13 Sit and Down Stays

My definition of stay is that when told to do so, my dog remains in the place and the position in which I left him, whether a sit, a down, or a stand. I am particular about this because of the requirements of the obedience ring. If my dog changes positions, say switching from a sit to a down, he fails the exercise. I also don't want him to move his front feet during the sit stay, or to shift from one hip to the other during the down stay, nor do I want him to whine or bark. I like to see a dog alert, yet relaxed and confident, while staying.

I strongly recommend that whenever you start any new stay proofing, you stand within 3 feet of your dog, with a leash connecting the two of you. I start with sit stay proofs. Though I don't always achieve it, the standard I train for on stays is no foot movement at all. Tail wags and head movements are okay up to a point. Often, they indicate that a movement error is about to happen, so be on the alert for errors if you start to see a lot of body movement during your stay training.

When teaching stays, I find that using both a positive marker—my CR—for success, and a negative marker—a verbal correction—for errors works best. When I first add distractions, I keep my leash short enough to snug it up immediately whenever my dog starts to move, but not so tight that he is unable to make a mistake. I want my dog to assume the responsibility for keeping himself in place.

While I don't insist that my dog maintains his attention on me during any of the stays—my eventual goal is to leave the area and go out of sight for Open stays—I certainly mark his attention on me with my CR when I get it, especially when I first introduce distractions.

Watch your dog closely to see where he's looking. Most mistakes start when your dog looks at a distraction, even if he doesn't actually break the stay and move toward it. Instantly mark any movement error with your voice—use your verbal correction—and snug up the leash to prevent an even bigger error. If your dog learned something from an earlier correction, he might still look at the next distraction but then should promptly look back at you. This is the attention you should mark with your CR and follow up with a treat. I love to see the dogs in my classes giving me disdainful looks when I attempt to distract them during a stay.

I introduce the following proofs to a sit stay. I have the owner apply the proof before I add another person. Once your dog can handle each of these proofs in a sit stay, do them during a down stay and a stand stay.

- Apply gentle, steady pressure forward on your dog's buckle or dead-ring choke collar—never on a prong or live-ringed choke collar—with your leash (Figure 13.1). Since most trainers are bigger than their dogs, most could move their dog when doing this proof. That isn't the purpose. You want to feel your dog resisting the pressure and solidly holding his stay. You may need to remind him to stay as you apply the pressure, or even put a restraining hand on his chest before applying the leash pressure. Verbally correct movement; CR and give a treat for success. As he masters minor pressure, build to stronger pulls that are not only straight forward but also off to either side. You can also pull on the leash or collar down toward the floor.

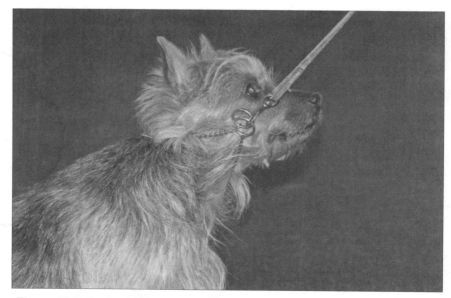

Figure 13.1: Apply steady pressure forward on your dog's collar with your leash. You are making use of your dog's natural *opposition reflex,* which causes dogs to brace against pressure. Note that the leash is attached to the dead ring (non-choking ring) of the collar.

Sit and Down Stays

The Exercises ❖ 47

- Apply gentle pressure on your dog's shoulders, rib cage, or thighs with your hand (Figure 13.2). If he moves, use an immediate verbal correction to mark his error, and try again. Use milder pressure if he keeps moving.

- Add pressure forward on his front legs when he is sitting (Figure 13.3). This may require a helping hand on the top of his shoulders. Many dogs have their weight unevenly distributed on their front legs. One leg feels like a metal post when you pull on it, the other a piece of limp spaghetti. Use your hand on the top of his shoulders, pushing down, to help him balance his sit better.

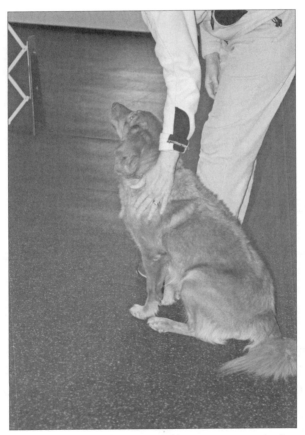

Figure 13.2: Apply pressure sideways on your dog's shoulders, rib cage, and thighs to test his commitment to the stay.

Sit and Down Stays

48 ❖ The Art of Proofing

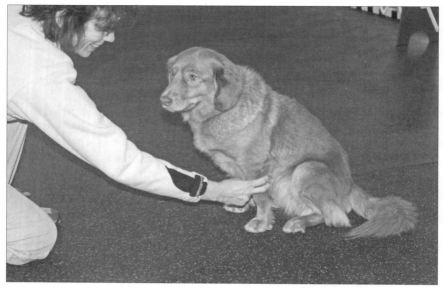

Figure 13.3: Corinne is applying gentle pressure to Neon's front leg. If your dog moves when you do this, use an immediate verbal correction to mark his error and then try again.

My progression of stay proofs with a helper is the same as the one I use during attention proofing. Tell your distracter what to do if your dog falls for a temptation and moves—she should back away while you reposition your dog, approach again, and repeat the same proof, perhaps with a bit less enthusiasm. Continue with that proof until your dog is able to resist the temptation, then move on to the next step.

- 👫 Distracter bends over nearby. I usually start about 8 feet away from dog and handler.
- 👫 Distracter bends over and pats her legs.
- 👫 Distracter bends over, pats her legs, and sweet talks your dog.
- 👫 Distracter moves in an arc back and forth in front of you, from one side to the other. She should be "nearby" for your dog, whatever that distance is. She should gradually turn the arc into a circle, with the circle getting smaller and smaller until it is within two feet of you and your dog.

- 👥 Distracter bends over and:
  - Extends her hand, with Phantom Food, i.e., she pretends to hold food in her fingertips but doesn't really.
  - Offers real food.
  - Offers a toy.
  - Waves a toy.
- 👥 Distracter drops a soft toy.
- 👥 Distracter squeaks a toy.
- 👥 Distracter crinkles a bag of treats.
- 👥 Distracter tosses a soft toy.
- 👥 Distracter squeaks and then tosses a toy (Figure 13.4).
- 👥 Distracter pets your dog.
- 👥 Distracter puts pressure on your dog's sides, legs, and thighs.

You also need to train your dog to maintain his stays in spite of any type of obedience exercise going on behind him, since stays are often done along gating with another ring beyond.

Some other distractions to proof against:

- 👥 Food getting dropped and rolling into the ring, such as a hotdog, a piece of a hamburger, or popcorn.

Figure 13.4: I squeaked and then tossed the ball and it was too tempting for Neon. Jet, Sparta, and Ranger all resisted me.

- 👥 Banging crates, with dogs going in and out of them.
- 👥 Someone setting up or taking down a metal crate.
- 👥 Someone dragging a crate dolly nearby.
- 👨‍👩‍👧 Dogs of very different sizes than your dog doing adjacent stays (Figure 13.5).
- 👨‍👩‍👧 Dogs of the same breed as yours in the stay line-up, since dogs are often especially excited by others of their breed.
- 👨‍👩‍👧 A nearby dog breaking his stay and wandering around. I simulate this in my classes by calling one of my dogs through a line of staying dogs.
- 👨‍👩‍👧 A breaking dog zooming around the ring.
- 👨‍👩‍👧 A breaking dog visiting your dog. I proof this in my classes by heeling one of my dogs around the dogs during stays. When they can cope with my dog in motion, then I add halts nearby.
- 👤 Practice waiting behind your dog as you return, to prepare your dog for a much slower handler returning next to you.
- 👤 Practice placing your leash and an armband number behind your dog while he is sitting facing forward, like you will have to do when you compete in an obedience trial (Figure 13.6).
- 👤 Practice retrieving your leash and armband and reattaching the leash before releasing your dog from his stay.
- 👥 While you practice sit stays, have someone do the Drop on Recall near your dog, using a loud verbal DOWN command.

Figure 13.5: It's important to work on stays with dogs of many different breeds. Note the armband numbers behind the dogs.

Figure 13.6: Colleen is practicing putting her leash and armband behind Ole as she will need to do when in an obedience trial.

- While you practice the down stay, have someone work on go-outs near your dog, using a loud SIT command.
- Have someone practice the Retrieve on Flat behind the stay line. The noise of the dumbbell hitting can cause errors.
- I do maneuvers around a staying dog with my dog in a stand. If the dog sniffs at my dog, my Flat-Coated Retriever whacks him in the face with his wagging tail, which serves as a correction (Figure 13.7).
- Expose your dog to someone in a wheelchair wheeling across the ring next to you and moving around on either side of your dog.
- Expose your dog to someone with a cane, a walker, or crutches.
- Practice extra long stays, since you don't want a judge's stopwatch malfunction to ruin your stays.
- Have your dog be a Figure 8 post while you stand 8 feet away as the other post (Figure 13.8). Do be careful to do this with a trustworthy dog.

Sit and Down Stays

52 ❖ The Art of Proofing

Figure 13.7: If Fire sniffs at Gryffin while we move nearby, Gryffin's wagging tail corrects him.

Figure 13.8: This group of handlers and dogs are positioned 8 feet apart in each direction. They are proofing their dogs' stays while Joy and Ranger are heeling around them as a distraction.

- Set the dogs up closer together than you need to for the ring.

Proofing the stays is critical not only for the group stays, but also on any of the exercises in which there is any distance between you and your dog, such as the Signal Exercise, which I address later.

Sit and Down Stays

14 Fronts

Your dog "fronts" on any exercise in which he comes to you, except the Utility *Moving Stand*. Ideally, he sits squarely and perfectly centered in front of you. The concept is relatively simple; the perfection is a long quest. Because fronts become more numerous as you move from Novice, with a single front, to Open with four, to Utility with six, fronts are a growing source of lost points when your dog is sloppy about them in the Open and Utility classes.

Figure 14.1: This dog is sitting in front position.

Work fronts:

- With selections discussed in *Categories of Proofs* (pp. 10-17) and *Adding a Person Nearby* (pp. 24-26).

- Past odds and ends on the floor, such as sticky dots, hair balls, or scraps of paper.

- With a person standing nearby, first behind you, then to one side, then the other.

- With a person walking up behind your dog as he comes into his front. This can happen on any recall. This can cause *automatic finishes,* which means your dog does a finish without a cue from you. Make sure your dog can not only front well enough with someone nearby, but can also stay in his front sit until you cue the finish. If he starts to finish without a cue, *don't* let him complete it—mark the error verbally and turn in place with him or block him with a hand or a foot.

- With someone dropping a toy nearby when your dog is 6–8 feet from you. This can cause your dog to skip his front. You want him to keep his focus on you all the way into his sit in front.

- With a person walking all around you as your dog fronts. A lot of dogs are especially startled by someone walking out from behind their handler, which often happens when a dog is returning to a front from a glove retrieve on the Utility *Directed Retrieve*, or after jumping during the Utility *Directed Jumping*.

- With your dog holding a dumbbell, scent article, or glove. A dog's ability to front accurately often deteriorates when he holds something in his mouth.

- While standing off to the side, so that your dog has to "find front." The farther your dog is from straight in-line with you, the harder this becomes. Most dogs are better at straightening their front from one side than the other, so you should spend more of your training time teaching your dog to master his harder side.

- With an object or a person blocking your dog's path. Start 6–8' away from the object at first. When he can adjust himself into a straight front properly, move closer to the distraction.

- With a toy or a cookie-loaded target behind your dog (Figure 14.2). If he is a thief, you'll need a helper or a leash to prevent him from cheating and stealing the treat early. Instead of stopping in front with his back to the toy or target, your dog might do an automatic finish and go right to heel so he can see where the toy or target is. When your dog successfully fronts, you can release him to the toy or treat as a reward. This is a great concept to teach young dogs in preparation for later Drop on Recall and Signal training and proofing.

- With your back near a baby gate or a wall.

- Standing at a 45° angle to a wall or gate (Figure 14.3).

- Leave your dog on a sit stay across from another person. Go stand to one side of that person—you are off center from your dog—and call your dog. Does he come to you or the other person? This is particularly important to work on with small dogs, who may not look up as high on your body as larger dogs. This becomes extra challenging if your helper dresses in clothes and shoes that are similar to your own.

Fronts

The Exercises ❖ 55

Figure 14.2: Use a loaded target behind your dog as a distraction.

Figure 14.3: Work fronts at a 45° angle to a gate or wall.

Finishes

56 ❖ The Art of Proofing

15 Finishes

When your dog "finishes" or "does a finish," he moves briskly to heel position, almost always from a sit in front. He can move around behind you to your right—sometimes called a circle finish—or move to your left in a swing finish, swinging his rear into place. Most dogs move their rear in a counterclockwise arc on the swing finish.

As with fronts, finishes become more numerous and thus more important as you advance through the class levels.

Work finishes:

- With odds and ends on the floor, especially behind you.

- Against a baby gate or a wall. Be sure to leave enough room for your dog to complete his finish.

- Against a baby gate with someone just outside tempting your dog.

- At a 45° angle to a wall or baby gate (Figure 15.1). Many dogs sit parallel to the mat, wall, or gate instead of straight in heel position. This is needed during the Utility *Directed Jumping.*

- With a dumbbell, an article, or a glove in your hand(s), i.e., practice with any of the items your dog needs to retrieve in the obedience ring. You need to figure out where you should hold each different object to get the best finishes. Some possible variations of where to hold the retrieve object include:

  - At your waist with both hands.

  - At your waist with your right hand, while your left hand is at your side. If this works best, practice taking the retrieve object from your dog smoothly with both hands, and while you lift it to your waist with your right hand, immediately return your left hand to your side.

  - Held at your right shoulder with the left hand hanging at your side.

Your dog's front may not be perfectly straight in the ring, so you want him to understand how to finish accurately from odd

Finishes

The Exercises ❖ 57

Figure 15.1: Work finishes at a 45° angle to a wall or baby gate. Many dogs sit parallel or perpendicular to the gate instead of straight in heel position.

places. Some dogs adjust their front instead of finishing when they aren't sitting in or close to a perfect front. Position your dog so he can perform an accurate finish from anywhere. Practice them with your dog:

- Standing in front of you.
- Sitting at an angle in front of you, varying the angle he starts from.
- Sitting, standing, or lying down in various locations around you.

Finishes

58 ❖ The Art of Proofing

✦ Practice finishes with your dog in positions that are pretty close to a perfect finish, since, if he does an automatic finish, some judges will still ask you to finish your dog.

Automatic Finishes

When your dog does an *automatic finish,* it means he does a finish without a cue from you. Sometimes the dog goes directly to heel position. I call these *drive by finishes.* Sometimes he does a sit in front, but then starts his finish without a cue from you. An automatic finish can be caused by the presence of a judge close behind the dog, making the dog feel uncomfortable. To escape the pressure of that close-up stranger, the dog finishes.

Make sure that your dog can stay in his front sit until you cue the finish. If he starts to finish without a cue, *don't* let him complete it—mark the error verbally and turn in place with him or block him with a hand or a foot.

✦✦ Work on your finishes with a person nearby, especially close in front of you. Review *Adding a Person Nearby* (pp. 24-26) for more ideas.

✦✦ Have someone repeat "Finish!" to make sure your dog waits for your command rather than going on the judge's command. Sometimes respond immediately, sometimes wait up to a count of 10. Instead of finishing him, you can circle your dog.

✦ Say "Finish" in many different voices when your dog sits in front. Sometimes follow it up with a finish cue, sometimes CR for waiting patiently.

✦ Twitch your shoulders or turn your head, but don't cue the finish.

✦ Alternate between calling your dog to a front and calling him to heel (as for the *Moving Stand*). Be clear with your cues—arms hanging at your sides for the front, using a hand signal along with the command for the call to heel.

✦ Vary how long you wait to give your finish cue. Sometimes do it quickly. Other times wait and reinforce the stay. Sometimes wait longer than usual and then finish him.

Finishes

16 Straight Recall and Drop on Recall

The Novice recall exercise requires you to leave your dog in a sit stay at one end of the ring while you walk to the opposite end, at least 35 ft. away. The judge, who might be quite close behind your dog, cues you with a verbal "Call your dog!" or with a hand signal, or sometimes both. Ideally, your dog gallops to you—a brisk trot is also fine—into a perfectly straight sit in front of you (discussed in the earlier section on *Fronts*). The judge then cues you to finish your dog, sometimes with a verbal "Finish" or "Finish your dog!" command, sometimes with a hand signal, sometimes with both.

On the Open *Drop on Recall*, the judge additionally cues you to have your dog down when he has come about halfway toward you on a recall. Judges usually cue you to drop your dog with a hand signal, typically by dropping or raising their hand.

You may start the following recall proofs even if your dog isn't yet able to do a Drop on Recall. In each case, you want to either drop your dog (once he knows how) next to the distracter or get him to come straight past her. If you don't have a person to act as your distracter, be creative and use toys or other objects that attract your dog's attention away from the recall.

Basic Recall Distractions

- As basic preparation for recall distractions, have your distracter stand beside your dog's path, about three feet to the side (Figure 16.1). A gregarious dog will typically go visit the person. When this happens, mark the error verbally, put him back where you originally left him, and try again. If necessary, have your distracter move farther away from your dog's path or move yourself closer to your dog to increase his chances of success. Once you

Figure 16.1: Colleen is ready to call Ole past me, standing about 3 feet to the side.

have corrected him a few times for visiting the distracter, your dog may respond by arcing away from the distracter on subsequent recalls. This is also an incorrect choice. Do what you must to show your dog that he is to come straight to you, whether you use a long-line, guides on the floor, or some other type of barriers to prevent the arcing. Food-toss recall games near the distracter will often help to reduce the arcing.

👥 Once your dog can handle the distracter standing alongside the recall path, have your distracter sit in a chair or on the floor nearby. For the overly friendly dog, ask your distractor to avoid eye contact with your dog (Figure 16.2). Then ask her to look at your dog (Figure 16.3).

Figure 16.2: I am avoiding making eye contact with Jet while sitting near her recall path.

Figure 16.3: I am looking at Dakota while sitting near his recall path. He's being a good boy and is ignoring me.

The Exercises ❖ 61

Once your dog is successful with a passive distracter, you can increase the level of distraction. Have your distracter:

- Stand next to the dog's path, bend over, and tempt your dog. Your distracter should start with voice and body motions such as leg patting. She can then move to Phantom Food, and advance to real food or a toy when your dog is successful with lesser distractions.

- Sit beside your dog's path, either in a chair or on the floor, and tempt your dog as in the previous example (Figures 16.4 and 16.5).

Figure 16.4: I'm in position with my tempting Phantom Food, ready to try to distract Jet on her Drop on Recall.

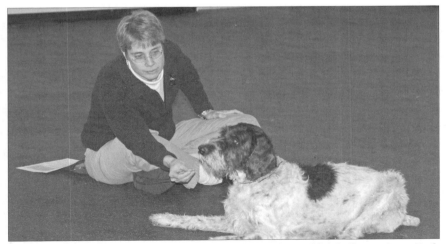

Figure 16.5: Jet is ignoring my attempts to distract her, which is the end result of enough proofing.

Straight Recall and Drop on Recall

62 ❖ The Art of Proofing

🚶🚶 Toss or roll a toy across your dog's recall path.

To proof the wait, i.e., against anticipation of your recall command:

🚶 Take a deep breath before calling. Sometimes just inhale, but don't call. Praise your dog for staying in place.

🚶 Use a nonsense command instead of your recall command, such as "apple", "taco", "sit", or "wait". Your goal is that your dog listens and stays in place until you use your actual command.

Have a friend stand to the side or behind your dog and:

🚶🚶 Motion with a hand signal for you to call your dog.

🚶🚶 Say, "Call your dog!" in various ways: softly, loudly, high pitched, low pitched.

🚶🚶 Move forward along with the hand cue.

🚶🚶 Run forward.

Refer to the *Sit and Down Stays* section for more ideas for proofing the sit stay.

Some proofs to work on when you are training by yourself:

🚶 Put a wind-up toy or a toy that will make a continuous noise for a short time off to the side of your dog. Gradually move the toy behind your dog.

🚶 Drop, toss, squeak, or kick a toy before you call your dog.

🚶 Drape a long toy or a leash across your dog's back and then call him.

🚶 Drop him alongside a high jump.

🚶 Drop him between a high jump and a broad jump.

Some proofs to do with someone else or in a group:

🚶🚶 One of my favorite Drop on Recall proofs is to have a friend stand about 6 feet to the side of where you leave your dog for the recall. The friend has a dumbbell, ready to throw it. She can also have her dog there to retrieve the dumbbell if desired. She says, "Call your dog!" to you. As soon as your dog starts on his recall, your helper immediately throws her dumbbell, of course trying to avoid hav-

Straight Recall and Drop on Recall

ing her dumbbell hit your dog ☺. Unless your dog is really slow on his recall, the dumbbell should land just about the time your dog reaches the midpoint and you cue your drop. Most dogs are initially caught off guard by this and fail to drop.

👪 Add a second helper to the previous proof. One person does the Drop on Recall, another does the Retrieve on Flat, and the third plays judge. When the judge says "Call your dog!" to the person doing the drop, the person with the dumbbell throws it. It should land just about as the recalling dog gets to the midpoint of the recall.

👪 Once your dog can successfully drop when a dumbbell lands nearby, make sure to also *not* drop him some of the time when a dumbbell lands nearby. I had to do a lot of straight recalls with my Border Terrier Java with someone tossing a dumbbell. He thought he was pretty clever after we worked through the "yes, you need to drop even when the dumbbell lands"—he started dropping anytime a dumbbell landed.

👪 Have two people stand about half way along your recall path, one on each side of the path, about 10 feet apart.

- Drop your dog between them.

- Have one of them hold a toy, motionless at first, then in more and more tempting ways.

- Have the two people play catch with the toy and drop your dog under the arc of the toy throw.

👤 Many judges mark where the stewards stand for the Figure 8 with chalk-mark X's or colored sticky dots. Since the Figure 8 is often along the path of the Drop on Recall, make sure your dog will do his recalls correctly in spite of the marks or dots.

UKC Drop on Recall

The UKC Drop on Recall is similar to the AKC version, but it adds a distracting steward. Once you've turned around to face your dog, who is in a sit stay at the other end of the ring, a ring steward steps to your side (Figure 16.4). After you have called and dropped your dog, the steward walks forward past your dog along a path parallel to your dog's path. Once the steward has passed your dog, the judge cues you to call your dog to front.

Judge

- 👥 Begin this by having someone stand near you when you do the entire Drop on Recall exercise. Just having another person near you may be enough to confuse your dog. Once he ignores your helper, then have her walk past your dog while he is in a down, waiting for your recall command. Have your helper vary the speed with which she walks past.

- 👥👥 Add a second helper so that you can have one play judge and one play steward.

Steward   Handler

Figure 16.4: a ring steward stands next to you on the UKC Drop on Recall until your dog drops, then walks straight forward until she passes your dog.

While the steward is usually at least two feet away from you, I once had one who stepped in so close that I felt like he was invading my personal space. Fortunately, it bothered me more than my dog.

To increase the difficulty, have your helper:

- 👥 Crouch down next to you instead of standing upright.
- 👥 Make brief eye contact with your dog as she walks past.
- 👥 Stare continuously at your dog as she walks past.

Refer back to *Adding a Person Nearby* (pp. 24-26) for more ideas.

17 Novice Stand for Exam and the Utility Moving Stand

When your dog does a *Stand for Exam* correctly, he keeps all four feet in place while the judge examines or touches him. The Novice exam is brief. The judge touches only the top of your dog's head, his shoulders, and his rump. You stand 6 feet away and your dog is off leash. The Utility *Moving Stand* exam is intensive. The judge touches your dog's head, ears, neck, shoulders, legs, rib cage, thighs, and tail. You stand 10–12 feet away during this exam, with your dog off leash. Judges do vary in their thoroughness on the Utility exam, some quite brief, some petting vigorously multiple times.

You are allowed to physically position your dog for the Novice stand. You should heel your dog into the Utility *Moving Stand* without hesitating. For the Novice stand, you return around behind and to heel position to complete it. For the Utility Moving Stand, you call your dog to heel with a verbal and/or a signal cue.

Heeling into the Utility Stand

- Review the proofs described in the section on *Heeling*.

- Have someone repeat the "Stand your dog!" command, to proof against anticipation. If your dog slows down or stops without you telling him to, remind him to heel and possibly add your leash for a while so that you can correct him for listening to the judge.

- Have someone crowd your dog during the heeling into the stand.

- Have someone move along with you after you have given your stop command.

- One person acts as judge. The remaining teams line up side by side. The judge calls "Forward" and "Stand your dog." Half the teams (predetermined who) stand their dogs and the others continue to heel. The judge examines the dogs who are standing, and cues each handler for the finish. Then swap who stands and who heels.

- Do the stand from a fast. Do this with caution. It may create stopping during a fast if you swing your arms a lot.

The Exam

Have many different people examine your dog in many different ways:

- Review and practice the proofs described in the *Sit and Down Stays* section.

- Approach from the front and to the dog's left.

- Approach from the front and to the dog's right.

- Approach from the side. Even though judges are supposed to approach from the front, they don't always do so.

- Walk rapidly towards your dog—swooping in for the exam.

- Do an exam with their fingertips, barely touching your dog.

- Examine your dog with extra heavy pressure on the top of his head, shoulders, and rump. Some dogs will sit for the rump pressure.

- Pretend to sniff, sneeze, or burp during the exam.

- Do a thorough, lengthy exam. Add in some sweet-talking for an extra layer of difficulty.

- Approach and put pressure on your dog's shoulders (from the side), rib cage, and hips (Figure 17.1). This is very helpful for the dog who moves his feet during the exam.

- Examine your dog while wearing a funny hat.

- Approach in an oddball way, perhaps tentatively, perhaps with a limp, perhaps very slowly, as an elderly judge might.

- Wear a long tie or jewelry that dangles on your dog during the exam.

- Tug on your dog's ears or tail.

- Pull forward on your dog's collar with a leash or a tab.

- Put pressure forward on your dog's legs or his rear end. This can cause your dog to move forward, which you don't want, so this is also a good method to help to proof against anticipation of the finish on the Moving Stand.

Novice Stand for Exam and the Utility Moving Stand

Figure 17.1: For a dog who moves his feet during an exam, have someone approach and put pressure on your dog's shoulders, rib cage, and thighs, all from the side. Your dog will learn to brace against this pressure and keep his feet still.

- Approach and start the exam before you have turned around to face your dog.

After the Moving Stand exam is done, most judges step back 4–6 feet directly behind your dog, and cue you to call your dog with a hand signal and often a verbal cue as well. Have a friend stand directly behind your dog and:

- Motion to you and say, "Call your dog to heel!" Make sure your dog holds his stay when this happens.

- Gesture with extra large arm motions and even some steps forward.

An efficient proof to use for the stand for exam in a class is to have half the class put their dogs "away"—crated, tied up, or on a down stay—so those without their dogs can act as judges.

- Position all dog and handler teams in a circle with all the dogs facing either clockwise or counterclockwise (Figure 17.2). Each handler stands their dog and steps in front. Then all of the "judges" circle in the opposite direction, everyone starting with a different dog, examining that dog,

68 ❖ The Art of Proofing

Figure 17.2: In a group setting, position all of the dogs in a circle, head to tail, for an efficient group stand for exam. Have half the group act as judges, proceeding from one dog to the next, approaching the dogs from the front, varying from which side the judges approach.

and then proceeding to the next one. Some people should approach from the left, some from the right. This provides many exams from many people in a short time. Once all the judges have examined each dog once, judges and handlers switch places.

The Moving Stand Call to Heel

- Review the proofs described in the *Finishes* section.
- Work the call to heel with distractions along the dog's path and with distractions behind your dog on the finish.
- Run forward once your dog is behind you on the circle finish.
- To build drive on your dog's return, have someone restrain him before you give your finish command.

18 Retrieve on Flat

When a dog retrieves correctly in the obedience ring, he stays sitting at your side while you throw your dumbbell. He leaves your side promptly on your command, moves briskly in a straight line to the dumbbell, picks it up cleanly without fumbling or kicking it, immediately turns without looking around or sniffing the floor or gate, and returns briskly to a sit in front of you, holding his dumbbell without mouthing or chomping. Although you will certainly lose points, you will probably still qualify on the exercise even if your dog does some chomping or drops it near enough to you that you can pick it up without moving your feet.

Retrieve Corrections for Errors Going to the Dumbbell

If my dog goes to a distraction instead of to the dumbbell, I mark the error verbally, then go to my dog, take him by the collar, take him to the dumbbell, which I pick up. I use a collar push toward the dumbbell and get the dumbbell in my dog's mouth. As my dog gains experience, I help less and correct more, changing from a mild collar push to a leash pop on the collar with the dumbbell on the floor. If I have taught my dog an ear pinch correction, I use that instead of the collar push or leash pop.

Retrieve Proofs

Since you cannot predict how clean the ring will be, train the following:

> Be sure to mark any errors verbally.

- Place a distraction—a toy, a piece of fluff, a Styrofoam peanut, a sticky dot— about 6 feet beyond the dumbbell (Figure 18.1). If your dog is very attracted to any of these distractions, place it beyond a baby gate so your dog can see it but not easily get to it. Work the retrieves with your dog on a leash if you need to prevent him from investigating the distraction. If you choose to use a physical correction, you should do so if your dog goes to the distraction instead of the dumbbell. However, if you introduce the distractions gradually, you will minimize the need for corrections.

- Gradually move the dumbbell closer to the distraction.

Retrieve on Flat

70 ❖ The Art of Proofing

- Position the dumbbell next to the distraction so that your dog has to go near the distraction in order to retrieve (Figure 18.2).

- Position the dumbbell beyond the distraction so your dog has to go past the distraction on his way to the dumbbell (Figure 18.3).

Once your dog has mastered each of the above distractions with various inanimate items, proceed with human distractions. Have a person stand 8–10 feet beyond the dumbbell. If your dog is excessively social, he is more likely to be successful if your distracter starts by standing there without any bending over, even looking at the ceiling if necessary. A social dog is easily drawn to eye contact.

The precise order in which you do the following proofs will vary, depending on whether food or toys are a stronger motivator for your dog. Use the weaker distraction first. The timing of when your helper adds the proof depends on which part of the retrieve needs proofing. Your helper can do each proof throughout the whole retrieve, can add it just before your dog arrives at his dumbbell, or just after his pick up.

To proof the retrieve, have your helper:

- Stand beyond the dumbbell, ignoring your dog.
- Make eye contact with your dog.
- Bend over, patting her legs.
- Add sweet-talking to the leg patting.
- Hold out Phantom Food.
- Hold out real food.
- Hold out a toy.
- Squeak a toy.
- Drop a toy.
- Toss a toy.
- Crinkle a bag of treats.
- Drop a bag of treats.
- Toss a bag of treats.

Retrieve on Flat

The Exercises ❖ 71

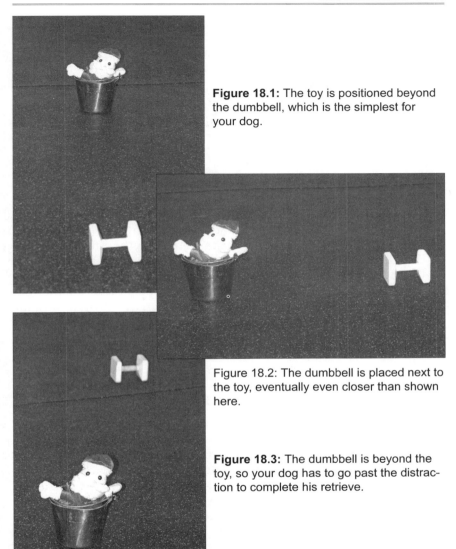

Figure 18.1: The toy is positioned beyond the dumbbell, which is the simplest for your dog.

Figure 18.2: The dumbbell is placed next to the toy, eventually even closer than shown here.

Figure 18.3: The dumbbell is beyond the toy, so your dog has to go past the distraction to complete his retrieve.

    Gradually shrink the distance between your dog and the distracter until she is tempting your dog by standing with your dumbbell between her feet. Complete the sequence with your distracter standing with a toe on an end of the dumbbell. That is a real test of your dog's commitment to his pickup.

Retrieve on Flat

72 ❖ The Art of Proofing

Next have your distracter sitting in a chair or on the floor 8–10 feet beyond the dumbbell. Repeat the sequence of distractions, gradually shrinking the distance between the dumbbell and your helper, completing it with your helper sitting with a finger, and then hand or foot, holding down an end of the dumbbell.

Next have your distracter stand beside the path from you to the dumbbell, and repeat the sequence.

You can also proof your dog's Retrieve on Flat in the following ways:

- Do the retrieve alongside a high jump. If your dog goes over the jump going out or returning, move farther away laterally from the jump, until he can retrieve correctly without jumping. Gradually move closer to the jump again. If this doesn't fix it, stand next to the jump and throw to the end of the ring (Figure 18.4) or throw the dumbbell even with the jump (Figure 18.5). Remember: simplify to succeed. Using a different command for the Retrieve on Flat vs. the Retrieve over High Jump should help your dog to differentiate between the two exercises.

- Do the retrieve between a high jump and a broad jump.

- Place your dumbbell on one end. Some dogs turn their head and grab the dumbbell, while others knock it over with their noses or foot and then pick it up.

- Place your dumbbell right in front of a baby gate. If your dog is afraid of baby gates and isn't brave enough to go close enough to retrieve his dumbbell when it is near a gate, you can desensitize him by throwing treats or a favorite toy near a gate. When he can easily get the treats from near a gate, resume working with his dumbbell. Start with it farther away and gradually move it closer to the gate.

- Add distractions beyond the gate, especially other dogs with their handlers (Figure 18.6). Sometimes, if there is a dog lying on the floor outside the ring, watching your dog approaching your dumbbell, your dog will give up because of the other dog's presence.

- Have a dog in a crate beyond a baby gate. If you don't have an extra dog to put in a crate, put a large stuffed toy in a crate instead. Once your dog is successful when the crate

Retrieve on Flat

Figure 18.4: Stand next to the high jump to prevent your dog from jumping on the Retrieve on Flat. When he succeeds, gradually move back to the end of the ring (to the left in the figure).

Figure 18.5: Place the dumbbell alongside the high jump to prevent your dog from jumping on the Retrieve on Flat. As he is successful, gradually place or throw it farther and farther past the jump.

Retrieve on Flat

is beyond the gate, position the crate within the ring, and go through the sequence described at the beginning of the section. I've used an airline carrier bag with a large stuffed animal sticking out, and placed my dumbbell right on the folded-down end flap.

- Place your dumbbell slightly under a baby gate, and then just beyond a gate. Normally, if your dumbbell lands outside of the ring, the judge will retrieve it and have you throw it again, but Treasure once dragged her dumbbell back under the gate in a trial in order to pick it up. The judge immediately told me he wouldn't deduct for the foot drag, since he had erred in ordering me to send her. Normally, if the dumbbell is within the ring, you get a point deduction if your dog touches or kicks the dumbbell with a paw.

- Prepare for a poor throw that the judge retrieves for you by having a friend retrieve the dumbbell for you. Judges normally say "Exercise finished" before they fetch the dumbbell. This means you may release your dog if you want. Practice to decide which is better: releasing or not releasing while the judge retrieves your dumbbell.

Figure 18.6: Neon is completing her retrieve in spite of all of the dogs and handlers on the other side of the baby gates.

Retrieve on Flat

One of my students was once ordered to send her dog even though her dumbbell was hanging on a baby gate. It was fortunate for the judge and the entire trial that her exuberant male Golden Retriever didn't pull down the whole line of gating when he successfully retrieved his dumbbell.

The following 5 exercises are used with permission from Margie English, and they are progressive. Don't do #5 until your dog can do 1–4 well. Margie devised them to help build up the retrieve memory for dogs who aren't natural retrievers. If you train a Sporting dog, the chances are these will be less of a challenge than, say, if you are training a terrier or a hound.

1. Leave your dog in a sit stay, walk forward, and place your dumbbell 10–20 feet away. Return to your dog. Send him to retrieve (Figure 18.7).

2. Throw your dumbbell. Turn a small circle with your dog to the left. Sit your dog in heel position. Send him to retrieve (Figure 18.8).

3. Leave your dog in a sit stay, walk forward, and place your dumbbell 10–20 feet away. Return to your dog. Turn a small circle with your dog to the left. Sit your dog in heel position. Send him to retrieve. This is a combination of #1 and #2. Don't combine them until your dog is consistently successful at both #1 and #2 (Figure 18.9).

4. Leave your dog in a sit stay, walk out, and place your dumbbell 10–20 feet away. Continue walking, and turn to face your dog 10–20 feet beyond your dumbbell. Cue your dog to retrieve. Some dogs run right past the dumbbell instead of retrieving it (Figure 18.10).

5. Leave your dog in a sit stay, walk behind him, and place your dumbbell 5–6 feet behind him. Walk back past your dog, turn to face him—it will look like a recall—and cue him to retrieve the dumbbell that is behind him. If placing your dumbbell right behind him is too challenging, progress more gradually, moving it from in front of him to the side and then behind him in stages (Figure 18.11).

Retrieve on Flat

Figure 18.7–Step 1: Place the dumbbell 10–20 feet from your dog, return, and send him to retrieve it.

Figure 18.8–Step 2: Throw the dumbbell 10–20 feet from where you are standing, turn a small circle to the left with your dog, sit him in heel position, and send him to retrieve.

Figure 18.9–Step 3: Place the dumbbell 10–20 feet from your dog, return, turn a small circle to the left with your dog, sit him in heel position, and send him to retrieve.

Retrieve over High Jump

The Exercises ❖ 77

Figure 18.10–Step 4: Place the dumbbell 10–20 feet from your dog, continue walking, turn to face your dog, and cue him to retrieve it.

 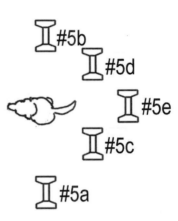

Figure 18.11–Step 5: Place the dumbbell to the side and then behind your dog, walk away as though for a recall, and cue him to retrieve. Since your respective positions will make it look like a recall, your dog may fail to retrieve the dumbbell. Help him to succeed.

Note: the dumbbells in the figures are not sized correctly for the dog ☺.

Retrieve over High Jump

19 Retrieve over High Jump

The *Retrieve over High Jump* is performed in a similar way to the Retrieve on Flat, but it has the additional requirement that your dog jumps over a high jump on his way out to retrieve the dumbbell and jumps again when he returns. The height of the jump is the closest multiple of two inches to your dog's shoulder height, between 8" and 36", with a few breed exceptions.

You must stand at least 8 feet from the jump. Most judges mark the floor or ground in some way to indicate this spot. Your dumbbell must land at least 8 feet beyond the jump. This distance is sometimes marked, too.

You will fail the exercise if your dog goes around the jump either on the way to the dumbbell or when returning to you. Since dumbbells can land unpredictably, whether due to your poor throw or an unlucky bounce, I believe that the most important proof for this exercise is to teach your dog to take the jump in both directions, no matter where the dumbbell lands. Practice this by throwing your dumbbell more and more off-center. Help your dog to succeed by using a hand in his collar to get him out to the jump if needed.

I like to see my dog focus his attention on the jump after he picks up the dumbbell, not look at me (Figure 19.1). I help him to look for the jump by stepping up closer to it, even tapping the center of the top board to show him where I want him to focus his attention (Figure 19.2). I don't add formality and stay in place farther from the jump until I see that my dog is consistently looking for the jump after his pickup, rather than at me.

Other proofs to train:

- Do all of the proofs listed in the *Retrieve on Flat* section, adding in the high jump.

- Put chalk marks or sticky dots 8 feet on either side of the jumps, as mentioned earlier. Many judges do this to mark the minimum distance you should stand from the jump, and the minimum distance you need to throw your dumbbell past the jump. These act like giant magnets for dog noses, so train for their presence.

- Hang a coat from one of the uprights.

The Exercises ❖ 79

Figure 19.1: Instead of looking at me, Ty focused her attention on the jump after she picked up the dumbbell that was far off to the left of the jump.

Figure 19.2: I help Ty to look for the jump by stepping up closer to it, even tapping the center of the top board to show her where I want her to focus her attention. I am stepping back away from the jump to give Ty space in which to land.

- 👤 Drape something over the top board of the jump.
- 👥 Have someone stand in various places around the jump. While most judges stand at the end opposite from you, some stand next to you or next to the jump.

Retrieve over High Jump

80 ❖ The Art of Proofing

⚫⚫ Have someone walk randomly around the area throughout the exercise. If your helper moves in toward the jump after your dog's dumbbell pickup, your dog might err and return around the jump instead, until he is confident about returning over it.

⚫⚫ Have a friend try to tempt your dog off-center after he picks up the dumbbell.

⚫ Place the jump diagonally across the ring, at a 45^0 angle to the sides of the ring (Figure 19.3). Since we have a judge in our area famous for setting up his ring this way, it is an important part of our training.

⚫ Place your dumbbell 8 feet beyond the jump. Once your dog can retrieve easily from there, place it even closer, in case a judge has you send your dog even when you haven't successfully thrown your dumbbell the required distance.

⚫ Place your dumbbell 8 feet beyond and well off to the side of the jump. If your dog turns to the right on his pickup, placing the dumbbell off-center to the right will be difficult for your dog. Be prepared for him to return around the jump, and move up if necessary to teach him the correct return path. Look for where your dog is focusing after he has picked up his dumbbell. He should be looking for the high jump, not you.

⚫ Set up a broad jump at the end of the ring beyond the high jump and throw your dumbbell near it.

⚫ Hang noise-making toys from the uprights and have them singing while your dog jumps.

⚫ Alternate between the ROF (Retrieve on Flat) and the ROJH (Retrieve over High Jump) to be sure your dog will do the appropriate one when you cue him (Figure 19.4). After a correct ROHJ, turn 90^0 to your left and throw the dumbbell for a ROF (position A in Figure 19.4). Gradually reduce the angle of your turn so that the dumbbell isn't that far off from where it is when you face the jump for a ROHJ. After he masters the ROF to the left of the jump, turn to the right of the jump, first 90^0, gradually reducing the angle as for the left side.

Retrieve over High Jump

The Exercises ❖ 81

Figure 19.3: Place a high jump at a 45° angle to the sides of the ring.

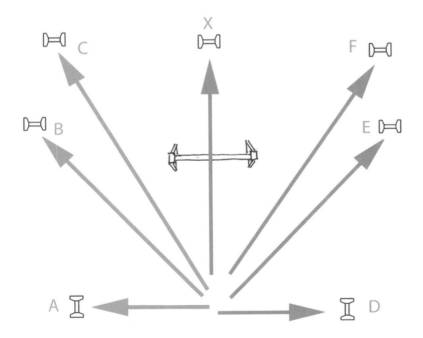

Figure 19.4: Alternate the ROF and ROHJ, starting with A–X, then B–X, then C–X. Once that side is going well, repeat the process with D–X, E–X, F-X.

Broad Jump

20 Broad Jump

The broad jump consists of two to four 8" wide, telescoping hurdles, with the tallest measuring 5 feet in length and about 6" at its highest point. These boards are arranged in order of height and are equally spaced, covering a distance twice that of the height of the high jump setting for your dog.

You need to position your dog at least 8 feet from the first hurdle. The judge usually marks the distance clearly, with a chalk line or a colored sticky dot on the floor, a piece of tape on the gate nearby, or a golf tee when on grass.

When you leave your dog, you walk to the right side of the jump, and stand with your toes about 2 feet from the boards (Figure 20.1). Again, most judges make some kind of mark to indicate where you should stand.

Ideally, your dog should jump over the center of the broad jump boards energetically, without touching any part of the jump, and without cutting the far right corner. While your dog is airborne over the jump, you turn in place to your right. Your dog should then turn back towards you, and move briskly into his sit in front.

Judges typically position the broad jump with its left side along one side of the ring. Think of all the different activities that could be happening just outside a ring—almost any of the obedience exercises; spectators; a conformation ring; vendors. Proof for them all. In addition, try the following:

- Place a distraction—a toy, piece of fluff, Styrofoam peanut, sticky dot, etc.—in various places in front of and beyond the jump.

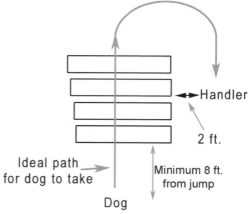

Figure 20.1: While not quite to scale, this shows the distances required and the ideal path for your dog to take.

The Exercises ❖ 83

- ♦♦ Have a person stand in various positions around the jump—directly across, 15–20 feet beyond the last hurdle, where many judges stand (Figure 20.2); on the left side of the jump, i.e. the opposite side from where you are standing; near you; and near the path the dog must take to jump.

- ♦♦ When your dog masters the standing person distractions, have someone sit in a chair or on the floor, in the same series of positions around the jump.

- ♦♦ Have someone run alongside the left side of the jump, as if she is heeling at a fast pace with her dog.

- ♦♦ Have someone do a recall with their dog alongside the left side of the jump, moving either away from your dog or toward him.

- ♦♦ Ask a friend to sit in a chair that you have placed just beyond some gating at the left side of the jump. When having someone sitting there no longer bothers your dog, have your friend stand up suddenly or talk with someone else. She might also have her dog with her, either lying at her feet or playing with a toy.

- ♦ For dogs who jump fewer than 4 boards, place the remaining board(s) near the left side of the jump.

- ♦ Place a folding ruler or a metal tape measure alongside the left side of the jump, as a way of preparing for the possi-

Figure 20.2: This is the typical set up for the broad jump, with the judge standing near the far end of the ring.

Broad Jump

84 ❖ The Art of Proofing

bility that a forgetful steward might fail to remove it after measuring the jump. I confess, I was that forgetful steward one time.

- When setting up the boards, set one or more up at a slightly skewed angle.

- When using 3 or 4 boards, vary the spaces between them, instead of making all the spaces the same.

- The set up place for the broad jump is often near the stewards' table, so you need to practice with a table, chairs, and people behind or next to your dog. If your dog needs to be more than 12 feet away from the jump to stride evenly to it, you may end up positioning your dog right next to the table or next to the exit of the ring. I normally use 8–10 feet for my set up point. I used 14 feet with my Flat-Coated Retriever Treasure for a while so that she would take three strides to the jump, but I fretted so much about her getting distracted by the stewards that I went back to 9 feet and two strides.

- Line up the left sides of the hurdles instead of the more typical right sides.

- Prepare for 2 of the 6 Open B orders by walking into a ring and starting with the broad jump. When I'm setting up for the broad jump I use my LOOK cue so that my dog knows that there is a jump in front of him.

- Send your dog to jump from different places than where you need to stand in the ring:

  - Anywhere between the first and last board.

  - On the left side of the jump, so your dog turns left after landing instead of right.

  - From the place you leave them, i.e., from heel position.

  - Standing 3–4 feet from the side of the jump instead of the required 2 feet.

Broad Jump

21 The Signal Exercise

Proofing the Utility *Signal Exercise* may be the most essential proofing that you will do to prepare your dog for obedience competition. After you have heeled a full pattern with him, you must stand your dog and then leave him alone at one end of a 50–foot ring, with the judge—a stranger—behind him. You walk approximately 40 feet away to the far end of the ring and then turn to stand facing him. Your dog is expected to ignore the stranger and distractions from adjacent rings, and, instead, pay attention to you and execute the signals—down from a stand, sit from a down, come from a sit—correctly, all with only hand signals from you. This is very difficult, and some dogs can get quite stressed on this exercise, but when done with animation, precision, and crisp responses, the Signal Exercise is simply breathtaking.

If you have shown in Utility, you have probably seen the "deer in the headlights" look from your dog during the Signal exercise. The dog's head is pointed directly at you, his eyes appear to be looking at you, you give your next signal... and nothing happens. The dog's body is in the correct position but his mind is not. Instead of focusing on the task at hand, he is thinking about the stranger behind him or what is happening in any adjoining rings, or simply may be too anxious about the fact that you abandoned him in such a scary place with a stranger nearby.

> Each time you introduce a new proof, decrease the distance between you and your dog.

As with all of your proofing, you should introduce what follows early in your dog's training. Don't wait until after you have started showing to discover that your dog freezes or is easily distracted on this exercise. Each time you introduce a new proof, decrease the distance between you and your dog.

As mentioned earlier in the section on *What You Will See In and Around the Ring* (pp. 15-17), you need to consider the background behind you, particularly during the Signal Exercise. If your clothing blends in with the background too much, your dog may have trouble seeing your signals (Figure 21.1). If you are backlit because of glare from a window or a suddenly opened door, you may appear as nothing but a silhouette to your dog. If your signals are too much in front of your body, the

86 ❖ The Art of Proofing

Figures 21.1: Wearing the dark sweater shown in the left photo helps me to contrast with the background better than the light shirt in the right photo.

glare may keep your dog from seeing them. If your dog depends on facial cues, how can he obey when he can't see those cues?

A lot of your signal proofing will need the help of a second person.

- Have your helper act as a judge and stand behind your dog. She should stand 10–15 feet away at first and then move closer as your dog learns to focus on you and ignore her.
- Have her stand behind your dog, giving you signals typical of judges, which are usually subtle hand motions with one hand and arm (Figures 21.2, 21.3, 21.4).
- Have her walk around behind your dog. Again, she should start at a distance and gradually move closer.
- Have your helper stand behind your dog while making large, sweeping motions, first with one arm and then with both arms (Figure 21.5).

The Signal Exercise

The Exercises ❖ 87

Figures 21.2: Judges typically use fairly subtle hand signals to cue you during the Signal Exericse. For the down, it is typically a small downward gesture.

Figures 21.3: For the sit, it is typically a small upward gesture.

- ♂♀ Have your helper wear a coat that will make noise when she moves her arm to signal you.
- ♂♀ Have her stand behind your dog, casting shadows that he can see. Be sure to reinforce your dog for ignoring the moving shadows.
- ♂♀ Ask her to train her dog nearby, throwing a dumbbell, doing recalls, heeling, and jumping.
- ♂♀ Have her deliberately distract your dog. She can squat down, pat the floor,

Figures 21.4: For the recall, it is typically a small forward motion.

The Signal Exercise

88 ❖ The Art of Proofing

Figures 21.5: Have a helper stand behind your dog making large, sweeping motions with both arms.

or hold out her hand. Start with Phantom Food (Figure 21.6), progressing to real food or a toy.

- Have her stand close to and eventually bend over your dog.
- Have her sit on the floor close to your dog.
- Have her crawl across the floor toward your dog.
- Have your helper stand straddling your dog (Figure 21.7). Use caution. This is usually a difficult and intimidating proof and most dogs creep forward to escape the pressure of the person standing over the top of them. If your dog starts to creep, move closer to him or use some sort of barrier to keep him in place.

The Exercises ❖ 89

Figures 21.6: Have your helper deliberately distract your dog. Here I am using Phantom Food to attract Ranger's attention.

Figures 21.7: I am straddling Neon as Corinne prepares to work signals. This is a tough proof for most dogs.

The Signal Exercise

👥 Have her toss or roll a toy across your dog's recall path. At first, she should toss the toy before you signal the recall. Later, she can do it just after your signal.

Other proofs to train:

- 👤 Sit in a chair or on the floor when you give your signals.
- 👤 Train your signals while wearing a variety of different clothes, such as a hat, a bulky coat, a raincoat, short sleeves, gloves, or sunglasses.
- 👤 Get a wind-up toy or a toy that will make a continuous noise for a short period of time. Put it off to the side of your dog and practice signals. Gradually move the toy behind your dog.
- 👥👥 Practice with a group of people standing at the end of the ring behind you (Figure 21.8) or behind your dog.
- 👥👥 Have several people clap and cheer after your dog responds to each signal. This simulates the happy, impressed John Q. Public crowd.

Figures 21.8: Corinne is practicing signals with a group of people and dogs gathered outside the end of the ring behind her. Notice how her clothes contrast with the background.

- 👥 Have several people walk around behind you or behind your dog during signals.
- 👥 Have the group wave their arms randomly, especially when they are behind you. Your dog might respond to their arm waves.
- 👥 Have someone pet your dog during the signals (Figure 21.9). Be careful. You don't want him to confuse this proof with the exam on the Moving Stand.
- 👤 If you are training alone, you can drop, toss, squeak, or kick a toy before giving a signal.
- 👤 Drape a long toy or a leash across your dog's back and work signals.
- 👤 Balance a toy on his shoulders and have him drop. Yes, most likely the toy will roll off. If he has completed the drop correctly, release him to retrieve the toy.
- 👤 Walk in an arc back and forth in front of your dog, giving signals at varying places in the arc and varying the distance between the two of you. Sometimes, I walk away and

Figure 21.9: I'm petting Ranger during the Signal exercise. Be careful that your dog doesn't confuse this with the Moving Stand exam.

The Signal Exercise

turn only partially around, and give my dog a signal. This way I can be sure he understands the hand signal itself without needing my body to be in perfect position.

- Place a target with a treat on it behind your dog (Figure 21.10). If he is a thief, you'll need a leash or a friend to serve as treat guard to prevent your dog from cheating and stealing the treat early. Drop him, then release him backward to the treat. Vary where in the Signal Exercise sequence you release him, at times waiting until after he does his sit in front or his finish. The backward release helps to reduce creeping toward you on signals.

- Glance away from your dog and then back to him, in the same way that you will when a judge is standing off to the side, giving you the signals.

- Wait up to a count of 10 between signals. Generally, you reinforce your dog for responding correctly to your signals, but this one proofs against anticipation. Sometimes, reinforce your dog for waiting in the current position before you give the next signal. Sometimes reinforce him for waiting a long time and then responding to your next signal properly.

- Just after you turn to face your dog, pause, and then turn a circle in place. Give your next signal and turn another circle.

- Have someone gently restrain your dog by the collar so he has to pull or push against the collar to perform the signals.

- Train your signals while a friend holds her hand near your dog. She should position her hand so that when you signal for a position change, your dog will bump into her

Figure 21.10: Place a target with a treat behind your dog to reduce creeping forward when you work Signals or position changes at a distance. Every so often, release him to go eat the treat.

hand as he responds. Many dogs hesitate or freeze when they feel the hand. When I do this proof for someone, I move my hand out of the way as soon as the dog hits it.

- For the down from a stand, your friend should hold her hand beneath your dog's chest or belly so he will bump into it when he starts to lie down (Figure 21.11).

- For the sit from a down, she should hold her hand just above your dog's shoulders so that he must push into it when he moves into his sit (Figure 21.12).

- For the recall signal, she should hold her hands in front of your dog's chest so he must push through them when he starts his recall (Figure 21.13).

Have your friend place her arms loosely around your dog's neck or body so he must push through the pressure to respond to your signals.

Work with a friend and her dog. Stand on parallel paths, facing opposite directions. You should each stand your dog and walk to the opposite end, each turning to face their own dog beyond where the other has left her dog. This puts you each in a position like a judge, behind and to the side of the dog. One of you signals her dog to drop, which serves as the signal to the other handler to drop her dog. Continue through the signals and then swap who signals first. If the dogs have trouble, move them farther apart laterally and don't go as far away.

Do the previous proof, but work with several handlers and dogs on parallel paths, alternating dog/handler/dog/handler. This really tests their focus.

Finally, be sure you regularly practice your signals in many different places.

The Signal Exercise

94 ❖ The Art of Proofing

Figures 21.11: For this down signal proof, I'm holding my hand beneath Ranger's chest. He'll bump into it as he lies down. As soon as he bumps into my hand, I move it out of the way.

Figures 21.12: For this sit signal proof, I'm holding my hand just above Ranger's shoulders. I move my hand out of the way as soon as he bumps into it as he sits up.

Figures 21.13: For this recall signal proof, I'm holding my hands just in front of Ranger's chest. I move my hands out of his way as soon as he bumps into them as he responds to the come signal.

Scent Discrimination

22 Scent Discrimination

The principal goal of the *Scent Discrimination* exercise is for your dog to find and retrieve an article that you have scented with your hands. You provide a set of articles. In UKC, you need 5 metal articles; in AKC, you also need 5 made of leather; in CKC, add 5 made of wood to the metal and leathers ones. Most exhibitors use articles that look like a dumbbell, although this isn't required. In the AKC Utility class, your dog must do the exercise twice, once to retrieve a leather article and once to retrieve a metal one. You may choose which type you scent first.

In the ring, the articles are supposed to be spread approximately 6" apart from each other. This arrangement is often called "the pile" even though the articles are not piled on top of each other. Most trainers refer to the pile as though it were a clock face, with 12:00 farthest away and 6:00 closest (Figure 22.1).

In AKC and CKC, you and your dog may watch the ring steward placing the lightly scented articles about 20 feet away from you. You then turn to stand with your back to the pile, your dog sitting in heel position. In UKC, your back is to the pile location as the ring steward puts them out. After you have scented your article, the judge or ring steward places it in the pile.

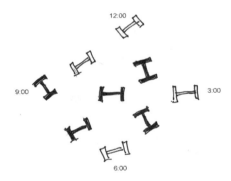

Figure 22.1: Most trainers refer to the article pile as though it were a clock face, with 12:00 farthest away from you and 6:00 closest.

I believe you need to be particularly careful when proofing scent articles. Your dog's job is to find the article that smells differently than the rest and return it to you. Proofing before your dog has a clear understanding of what his job is may add too much stress for your dog and create big problems with the exercise. Although I want my dog to learn to work under duress, some proofing that is too difficult too early in the training of scent discrimination may confuse him into making a lot of mistakes. Above all, work to build your dog's confidence. Don't be afraid to reduce the number of articles or to shorten your distance from the pile.

I recommend the following proofs:

- Start with the proofs listed under the *Retrieve on Flat* section.
- Place articles near a jump.
- Place articles near a baby gate.
- Use extra articles in the pile to make your dog search longer.
- Place one article, either the one you have scented or a different one, a short distance away from the pile. This is important for dogs who scatter articles because of their method of working the article pile.
- Work the articles so the path to and from the pile is parallel to the jumps (Figure 22.2). This is especially important if you use the direct send to the pile, a.k.a. the flying send. I've seen dogs who are sent this way go over a jump instead of going directly to the pile.
- Place all of the articles in a straight line. You can use many variations, including the place within the line, the direction of the line, and the direction of the articles within the line.
- The regulations say the articles should be placed about 6" apart, but since stewards don't always accomplish this when they set out your articles, train with articles that are either very close together or very far apart.

 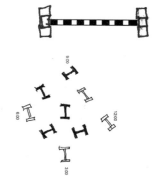

Figure 22.2: This dog is incorrectly going over the high jump instead of going to the article pile.

Scent Discrimination

- Arrange the articles in different orderly configurations, such as different letters, circles, squares, triangles, etc.

Don't attempt the following proofs until you have worked through similar ones with your dumbbell retrieve.

- Have a friend stand close to the pile. When your dog works well with a person near the articles, add a dog near the pile.

- Have a friend sit close to the pile in a chair or on the floor.

- Set up an X of baby gates (see Figures 11.3 and 11.4 in the *Heeling* section, pp. 38-39). Put an article pile in each of the four areas defined by the gates (Figure 22.3). Have four teams working articles at the same time.

- Have a friend stand in the pile, with articles all around her feet.

- Have her sit in the pile, with articles all around her.

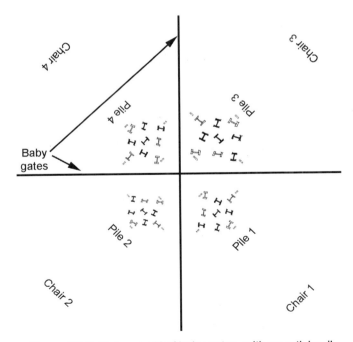

Figure 22.3: Set up an X of baby gates, with an article pile in each of the four corners defined by the gates. Have four teams working articles at once.

- 👥 Have your helper sit in the pile with the correct article up on her leg.

- 👫 Set up four chairs close together, each facing out in a different direction (Figure 22.4). Have four people working articles at the same time.

- 👤 Put novel objects near or in the article pile. They should not be edible, just different enough to warrant investigation, such as a toy or small scraps of paper. First place those new items beyond the pile, even on the other side of a gate if you know they are a huge temptation to your dog. Gradually move the distraction closer to the pile.

- 👤 Put distractions along the dog's path to the pile. Vary where along the path you place them.

- 👤 Put a colander with food under it near the articles.

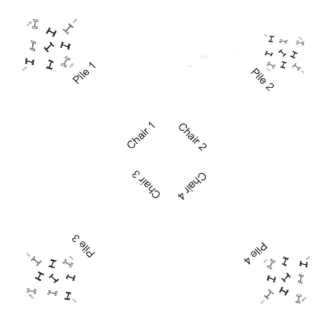

Figure 22.4: Set up four chairs close together, each facing a corner. Have four teams working articles at once.

The Exercises ❖ 99

♦ Put an article or two on end. This is important for a dog who works fast and scatters articles in the process.

♦♦ Have someone drop a dumbbell nearby just as your dog gets to the articles. When your dog succeeds with this proof, have your helper toss a dumbbell. Have another dog retrieve that thrown dumbbell to add another layer of difficulty.

♦ Have someone give extraneous commands while your dog is scenting the pile.

♦♦♦ Have a burst of applause while your dog is working the pile.

♦ Have someone squeak a squeaky toy at various points during the exercise. You can even do this yourself.

♦♦♦ Place 1–3 articles—enough to make a clear pile—from several different people's article sets in the center of the training area. It's ideal if there are different kinds and sizes. An extra person should scent all of the central articles. Each person then places one of their scented articles in the pile. The most advanced dog should work first, working down to the least experienced dog. The working dog has to find not only a hot-scented article (assuming the handlers use hot scent) but also the one that smells like his handler.

Make sure you know the correct response to the judge's question: "What method will you be using to send your dog?" The correct responses are either **"After a sit."** or **"Send directly."** I have always used the "after a sit" method with my own dogs, because I feel it gives me more control of where my dog goes. For those who use the "send direct" method, a distraction that happens in the midst of your turn to the pile might cause your dog to pause and require another command to go, which would be an NQ, so make sure your dog can cope with a variety of distractions during your turn.

Scent Discrimination

23 Directed Retrieve

In this Utility exercise, you and your dog stand at the center point of a 40 foot X 50 foot Utility ring with your backs to one end (Figure 23.1). A ring steward then places three gloves behind you, along the end. The judge tells you by number, and often a hand gesture, which glove your dog should retrieve. You must pivot in place to face the glove, and you may pivot in either direction. Your dog should maintain heel position throughout your pivots. Once you have finished the pivot, you then give a signal with your left arm and hand along the right side of your dog's head, along with a verbal cue to go retrieve the glove you are indicating. Once your dog picks up the glove, he should return to a sit in front of you as in the Retrieve on Flat.

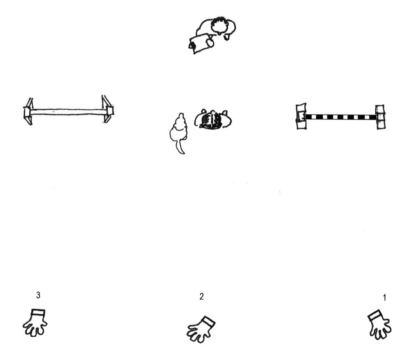

Figure 23.1: While not quite to scale, this diagram shows the numbering of the gloves when they are behind you. Note: the handler stands at the midpoint of the ring, centered between the jumps.

Directed Retrieve

I suggest the following proofs:

- First review the proofs listed in the *Retrieve on Flat* section.

- Teach your dog to follow your hand signal when you are not actually facing the glove that he is to retrieve. Place two gloves about six feet away, one glove to your right and one to your left. You and the two gloves should form an equilateral triangle (same length sides) (Figure 23.2). Face the midpoint between the two gloves, rather than directly toward one of them, but vary which one you send your dog to retrieve. Be sure your signal points to the correct glove.

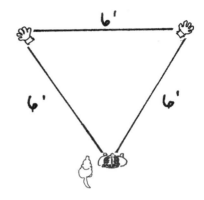

Figure 23.2: Face the midpoint between two gloves and vary which glove your have your dog retrieve.

- Face one glove and have your dog mark and retrieve the other glove. As with the previous proof, be sure your signal points to the correct glove.

- Put three gloves in a line extending away from you (Figure 23.3). Have your dog retrieve the closest one, then the next one, and finally the farthest, without replacing retrieved ones. You can include a pivot if you wish. This can help to extend the distance your dog will go to retrieve a glove. I don't care if my dog retrieves a farther away glove before the closest one.

Figure 23.3: To help extend the distance your dog will go to retrieve a glove, place 3 gloves in a straight line away from you.

102 ❖ The Art of Proofing

- Do the previous proof with 9 gloves, 3 on each line to the normal glove locations. Have your dog retrieve them in a random order.

- Place your gloves:

  - Near a patch of sunlight (Figure 23.4).

  - In a patch of sunlight (Figure 23.5).

  - Against a white background (Figure 23.6).

- Teach your dog to do a blind retrieve, especially if you are planning to show him outdoors where gloves can easily disappear in tall grass or in a small dip in the ground. In a blind retrieve, you send your dog to retrieve a glove that he may not see until he is nearly upon it. Initially teach this with one hidden glove. Once he reliably retrieves a hidden glove, you may add visible gloves as well. Start by only sending him to the hidden glove and not the visible gloves.

- Have a decoy glove off to the side but closer to you than the correct one. Start with the decoy to your right, so you can block your dog's view of it with your signaling left hand.

- Have someone stand by the correct glove.

- Have someone stand by an incorrect glove.

- Have a friend move around the ring nearby. This is important to proof for because, after judging the initial pivot to the glove, the judge must walk around from behind you so that she is in front of you to judge your dog's front. While some judges are unobtrusive when they do this, others are not. The judge's movement might push your dog over the jump or into an automatic finish.

- Work the gloves with the jumps in place, to proof against your dog taking a jump on his return to you. Start with the jumps the normal 18–20 feet apart that they are in an AKC trial, and then gradually move them closer together. This proofs against your dog jumping on his return.

- Have your dog retrieve a glove from a gated corner (Figure 23.7).

- Have your dog mark a glove that is four to six feet away from you, closer with a small dog, farther with a medium

Directed Retrieve

The Exercises ❖ 103

Figure 23.4: Place your gloves near a patch of sunlight. Many dogs will go to the sun patch instead of their glove.

Figures 23.5: Place your glove in a patch of sunlight, which makes it harder for your dog to see it.

Figure 23.6: Positioning a glove against a white background such as this wall makes it harder for your dog to see it.

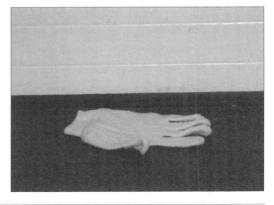

Directed Retrieve

Figure 23.7: Ranger is fetching his glove from a gated corner.

to large dog. Toss a decoy glove off to your right just after you give your mark signal. The goal is for your dog to ignore this distraction and maintain his mark on the correct glove. You can toss this decoy yourself or have a friend drop it for you. Once your dog succeeds in ignoring a glove tossed to your right, toss a decoy glove to your left, either over your dog's head or under his chin. Advance to tossing a decoy after your dog has left your side to retrieve the one you pointed to. Start close to the correct glove, with the decoy tossed farther away. Gradually reverse their respective distances.

- Have someone stand very close to you, next to your side, as your dog comes back with the glove to sit in front. This will test whether your dog will try to front to the judge instead of you, as well as his ability to front accurately.

- Place several gloves in a circle or square, and stand with your dog in the center (Figure 23.8). After each correct retrieve, return that glove to its place and pivot to your left—counterclockwise—to the next glove. It is easier when you pivot to your left because you can block your dog's view of the previously retrieved glove when you use your left arm and hand to point to the desired glove. After your dog has

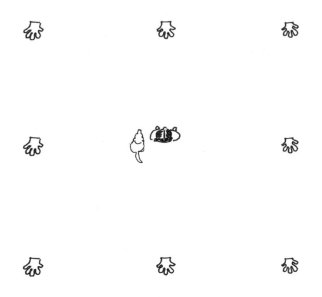

Figure 23.8: Stand in the middle of a square of gloves. No matter which side you face, there are always corner gloves. The presence of the other side gloves makes the corner retrieves more challenging.

mastered pivoting to the left, pivot to the right (clockwise). You can then pivot and send your dog to random gloves.

- Add two small white objects in between the regular glove positions. I have some small gloves made of wood and painted white. I also use these in place of a regular glove for a dog who insists on going to a wrong glove. Most are very surprised when they attempt to retrieve the wooden glove.

- Work with your gloves against gating when there are various activities going on beyond it: heeling, recalls, retrieves, spectators, other gloves, or a jumping dog. Have spectators standing or sitting in chairs with their dogs.

- Face your dog toward a glove that is 6–8 feet in front of you. Attach a retractable leash (a.k.a. a flexi-lead) to a decoy glove. Position this decoy glove 6–8 feet to the right

Directed Retrieve

of the glove you are facing, so that you can block your dog's view of the decoy with your left arm and hand. Have a friend slowly retract the leash, dragging the decoy glove across the floor toward her, while your dog marks the correct one (Figures 23.9–23.11). While this sounds hard for your dog, it is so obvious that most dogs quickly learn to

Figures 23.9–23.11: The top picture shows the setup for the "glove on a flexi" proof. As Corinne gives Neon the mark signal for the glove (top), I start slowly retracting the decoy glove. The photo on the right shows how to attach the flexi to the glove. To slowly retract the glove, the helper should hold the cord between her fingers of one hand while controlling the flexi with the other (bottom).

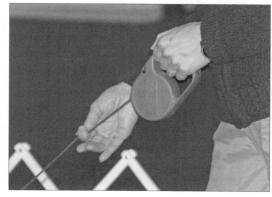

ignore it. There are many variations of this exercise. Your friend can drag the decoy toward a corner, toward the center, away from you, toward you, and so on. Once your dog ignores the decoy consistently when it is on your right, switch the decoy to your left.

- Practice the ring set up, with a judge standing 5–6 feet in front of you and a steward moving behind you, placing your gloves.
- Set up an X of baby gates (Figure 23.12). Put a glove in each of the four areas defined by the gates. Have four teams work gloves at the same time. Each person may move around their area to change the angle of the turn required to face the glove.

Figure 23.12: We're using the X of baby gates set up. We've each put a glove in the four central corners and have four teams working gloves at the same time. Even if you don't have as many as four teams, simply putting extra gloves in the other corners will provide distractions.

Directed Retrieve

24 Directed Jumping

In the part of the Utility *Directed Jumping* exercise commonly known as go-outs, you stand at one end of the center-line of a 50–foot ring, with your dog sitting in heel position. The high jump and bar jump are set up, one on each side, 18–20 feet apart and 25 feet from the far end of the ring. The judge chooses which jump is on which side (Figure 24.1).

For a perfect go-out, your dog must move briskly in a straight line away from you, towards the center of the opposite end of the ring. On your command, he should turn in place and sit without walking forward, while keeping his attention focused on you. You want your dog to sit about 20 feet beyond the jumps, about 5 feet from the end. You are allowed some leeway—a couple of feet either way—but this is the place you should aim for. When a dog sits at the end of the go-out, it is ideal if he turns in place without making an arc and sits facing you. You are not marked off if your dog sits crookedly, but it will be easier for him to get to both jumps if he faces you.

In the second part of the exercise, once your dog is sitting at the opposite end of the ring, the judge will instruct you to send your dog to either the high jump or the bar jump. You may use a voice command and/or a hand signal to cue your dog to take the jump.

When your dog is airborne over the jump, you may pivot to face him if you want to. Your dog should come into a sit in front, and then finish when so cued.

To complete the exercise, you send your dog on another go-out and direct him over the other jump.

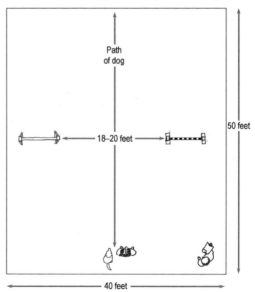

Figure 24.1: The set up of the ring for Directed Jumping.

Go-outs

Go-outs, like fronts, are a simple concept to us humans. I could teach a child of 5 to do decent go-outs in about 5 minutes. Unfortunately, it takes a lot longer to explain it to our dogs. I think one of the missing pieces for most beginning Utility dogs is lack of adequate repetition on go-outs. I've had many people come to me for help with their go-outs, and when I ask them how many they do in a training session and over the course of a week, they pause to give it some thought, and then say maybe four a day, 2–3 times a week. This is rarely enough. Nancy Patton used to say it takes several thousand repetitions for most dogs to understand go-outs. Judy Byron used to say it takes about a million reps. I think somewhere in that range is probably accurate.

Dogs err on go-outs in several common ways. They may veer off the center line, resulting in a deduction ranging from a few points off to an NQ (non-qualifying), depending on the path taken. They often stop short—points off to an NQ, depending on how short and how the handler reacts. They don't sit promptly—points off. They don't sit at all or they lie down—3 points off. Or they take a jump on a go-out—an NQ. I have experienced every one of these problems with each of my dogs with whom I have competed for any length of time.

Departing from the rest of this book, I'm including how I train go-outs. In part, this is because I have expanded on what I do since *Competition Obedience: A Balancing Act.* In part, I want to provide an easy-to-take-along reference, since go-outs require so much training away from home.

Go-out Props

When I first introduce go-outs, I use broad jump boards to make a chute to help guide my dog to take a straight path. My dogs are introduced to these guiding boards during several other exercises (backing up while facing me, food-toss recalls through the boards, and fronts with guides), so they are familiar with them when we start go-outs (Figures 24.2).

I also teach go-outs using a plastic lid that most dog trainers call a *target*. Before starting go-outs, I teach my dog to touch one of his front feet to the target. This helps to make the target an attractive destination for my dog before I ever start go-outs formally.

Directed Jumping

Figure 24.2: This shows a Utility ring setup with two sets of broad jump boards used as guides.

As my dog progresses in his training, I reduce the size of the props, going from broad jump boards to long skinny sticks (Figure 24.3), to carpenter's chalk lines (without the chalk) stretched the length of the ring (Figures 24.4–24.6). I shrink the size of the target and change from a white one to a red or green one. I've had students who ultimately use a coin as their target.

I will also transfer the foot touch from a target to a plain wall or the stanchions that hold up the baby gates. Many trainers teach an automatic touch, so that if they don't give their sit command, the dog should touch something at the end of the ring. This helps to reduce the stopping-short syndrome. During the last year of Java's trial career, I made this switch. Initially, I would send him with GO-OUT, and as he neared the end of the ring, I'd either command SIT or TOUCH. Then I eliminated the touch command and waited for him to touch on his own, which he did by standing on his hind legs and putting his front feet up on the side of a stanchion. Based on my experience, you do need to make sure to balance your use of the automatic touch and your sit command. We had some substantial point deductions in Utility trials when Java ignored my sit command and touched the stanchion before sitting.

When I introduce a new proof, which might simply be training my go-outs in a novel location, I back down the go-out staircase and add back in some props to help my dog succeed. In the explanations that follow, I refer to "the target." This can be whatever you use to help your dog do his go-outs correctly. It might just be guides at the end of the ring. It might be a target with a treat. It might be a sticky dot on the wall.

Directed Jumping

The Exercises ❖ 111

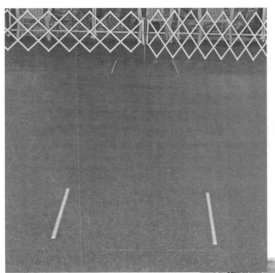

Figure 24.3: Here are two sets of long sticks used as guides.

Figure 24.4: The two carpenter's chalk lines are attached to the gates at the far end. With practice, you or a helper can lift up on one if your dog veers off line in that direction. The bottom picture shows the setup for a dog who veers to the left, with the left line already lifted.

Directed Jumping

112 ❖ The Art of Proofing

Figure 24.5: Always attach the chalk lines near the bottom of your baby gates. Otherwise, you might pull the gates over and spook your dog.

Figure 24.6: I added a small clip to the end of my chalk lines to simplify attaching them to the gates.

Directed Jumping

The Exercises ❖ 113

Taking the Go-out on the Road

Much of your early teaching was probably done in a familiar area. A lot of your proofing must be done in new locations. When you first go to a new place, you may need to back up a few steps in your training to be sure your dog has a reasonable chance to succeed.

Before you take him out to train, put out your target without your dog seeing you do so. Begin at the new location about six feet from the barrier and target. This barrier can be a wall of a building, a baby gate or two that you have taken with you, a baseball backstop, a tennis court fence, a tree, or even a stake in the ground. Whatever you use will help to show your dog that the go-out has an end.

Lengthen your distance from the target and repeat until your dog is able to do a straight go-out from 50 to 60 feet away from the barrier. Repeat the go-out exercise 10 to 15 times in this new location, placing food randomly on your target if you use it.

The next day, return to the same location. Set out your target, again without your dog seeing it. Get your dog out and start the go-out from six to eight feet away from the target. If your dog goes properly, run to him and have a celebration. If not, move closer or take him out and show him what he missed.

Continue to visit this same new location every day, starting a little farther from the target each time.

At some point, you must try the first go-out and then the first two go-outs without food or a target in place. Eventually, your dog will do the first two go-outs perfectly without food or a target, starting 50–60 feet from the now familiar barrier. You must then move to another new location and start the same procedure all over again.

Vary the background to which your dog runs, and eventually add people and dogs beyond the end of the go-out on the other side of the gate, as if you were at a dog show. There are times when there will be another dog working in the adjacent ring, so proof for that as well. Have people and dogs sit along the side of the ring, too.

Perfecting go-outs is a long process but very much worth it to get that wonderful Utility Dog title.

Directed Jumping

General Go-out Tips

Train them in many, many different locations. Repeat them a lot. Early in my dog's go-out proofing, I don't set up jumps, which simplifies the process immeasurably.

Have two targets at opposite ends of your training area. After sending your dog on a go-out to one, drop a treat on the target behind you. Do this while your dog is still moving away. Run out to your dog after the sit, reward him if desired, and send him the other way to the target you just loaded.

> If your dog makes the same mistake twice in a row, change something—most likely simplify somehow—since he will almost undoubtedly make the same mistake a third time.

Solutions to Common Go-out Errors

As I've mentioned before, you should expect errors when you introduce proofing to any exercise. You should also have some plan of how you are going to react when your dog makes different types of errors. My normal go-out correction is to take my dog by the collar and run him along the ring's center line all the way out to the correct spot at the end of the ring, repeating my go-out command. With an experienced dog, I might simply say, "No, GO OUT!" Here are some general ideas of how I handle typical errors:

Veering off the center line: I stop my dog with my verbal correction as soon as he veers. I take him by the collar back to the center line, just before the spot where he started to veer. I then take him out to the correct spot, repeating my go-out command. With a small dog, I might attach my leash so I don't have to bend over to hold his collar. If my dog continues to veer, I add back in the guides I used when first starting to teach go-outs.

Stopping short: I stop my dog in different places along the path, so he learns to listen to my command, rather than sitting where he thinks he should stop. I expand on this in the upcoming section on *Proofing Against Stopping Short*.

Taking a jump on a go-out: Nowadays, when trainers run into this problem, they blame it on agility. My early dogs, who never did agility, all figured out that taking a jump on a go-out was a possibility! It's just one of those things that most dogs try at some point. For a dog who seems to try this option frequently, I take the bull by the horns and alternate sending him to a jump from the go-out launching pad and sending him on a go-out. I use a step towards the jump along with a hand signal given with my palm up (Figure 24.6). When I use a signal on my go-out send, my palm is facing my leg and my signal is straight forward (Figure 24.7). When I send to the jump on my right, I do start my dog on my right instead of in heel position. On the next go-out, my dog is back in heel position.

As mentioned before, I add back in some props if my dog is confused, to help reduce his errors. I might move closer to the center point of the ring to send my dog on his go-out, gradually backing up to the official launching pad.

When my dog doesn't go where I want him to, I stop him with a verbal correction and call him back (NO, COME.), and try again. If he repeats the error right away, I simplify some more.

I have found with most of my dogs that they are quite honest about going where they are looking, so building a strong mark on the end of the ring helps me know where my dog will go.

Figure 24.6: Belinda is cueing Sparta to take the jump on their left by stepping toward the jump and motioning with her left palm up.

Figure 24.7: Belinda is cueing Sparta to go out by motioning with her left hand held with her thumb up, palm facing right.

116 ❖ The Art of Proofing

Poor sit on go-out: This can take several forms, from a slow sit, to a creeping forward sit, to a no sit or lying down. These are all symptoms of a poor sit. You might use guides of some sort to better define the place your dog should sit. Make sure your dog is capable of sitting promptly with you nearby. If he creeps a couple of inches when you are only 4 feet away, this usually becomes a much larger distance when you are farther away.

Food-Toss Sit

To train the go-out sit, I do an exercise I call *the food-toss sit*. I start this early in my dogs' training. I use a 6–foot leash initially. I stand my dog facing me, about 3 feet away. I say SIT, and observe how my dog sits. Does he sit promptly? Does he stare blankly at me? Does he take any steps forward with his front feet? If so, I immediately step towards him and lift up on the leash to prevent any additional steps. I don't advance to the next step until my dog will sit promptly in place with me 5–6 feet away, still holding the end of the leash.

Once this criterion is met, I start the cookie-toss portion. I hold several treats that will be visible when tossed on the surface on which I'm working. (This doesn't work well in grass.) I toss a treat 3–4 feet to one side of my dog, along with a GET IT command. As soon as he has eaten the treat, I command SIT. If he sits promptly, I use my CR to tell him he's right, and then repeat the treat toss, GET IT, SIT sequence. If he doesn't sit promptly, I'll use my leash to correct him, or step towards him to prevent creeping forward. If the tossed treat bounces farther away than expected, move! Don't stand there with cement shoes on. Follow your dog as he chases the treat until you are at your current working distance. As his responses improve, gradually increase the distance you throw the treat. The cookie tosses help dogs learn to sit promptly in place, since the fastest way to the next cookie is not to run back to you, but to sit quickly.

For a particularly fast sit, I walk to my dog and give him a treat, or even several if it was brilliant. For a particularly slow sit, I do not toss a treat, but instead turn to the side to release my dog, and then again cue the sit.

I've had several students, not to mention my own dogs, whose dogs first learned a distance sit with this exercise. Folding it into a go-out was a simple matter.

Directed Jumping

The Exercises ❖ 117

General Go-out Proofs

- Place enticing things just outside the end of the ring and off-center, such as a chair, toys, your training bag, or a favorite dog buddy. This is likely to create a crooked go-out.

- Have people and dogs outside the gates at or near the go-out spot. This might cause your dog to avoid the spot, or it might cause him to sit slowly or not at all.

- Toss food or toys into a corner a few times for the dog to eat or fetch, and then do go-outs. I recommend that you start this in the learning stages when you still have your target out. I elaborate on this type of proof in the section *Gloves and Go-outs*.

- Fluff proof the go-outs, especially for small dogs, who love to stop at any bit of fluff on the floor on the way to the go-out spot.

- Roll or throw a toy over his head or past him while he is running. This is very challenging for most dogs.

- When you have a helper, have her throw a toy across your dog's path.

Proofing the Sit

- Working with a partner training her dog in an adjacent ring, both of you send your dog toward a central ring gate, so your dogs are running at each other (Figure 24.8). Often, the slower dog will sit when he hears the faster dog's handler say SIT.

- Roll a ball so it is still rolling when you command the sit at the end of the go-out. You can do this yourself or have a friend do it for you.

- Follow your dog part way out on the go-out. Stop as or just before you call for the sit, and start walking slowly backward. Many dogs will creep forward when you do this. Start close to your dog, gradually increasing the distance between you and your dog, and the speed with which you run backwards. If this creates a lot of errors—usually creeping or failing to sit—train this outside of the go-out context by adding this to food-toss sit games, which allows

Directed Jumping

118 ❖ The Art of Proofing

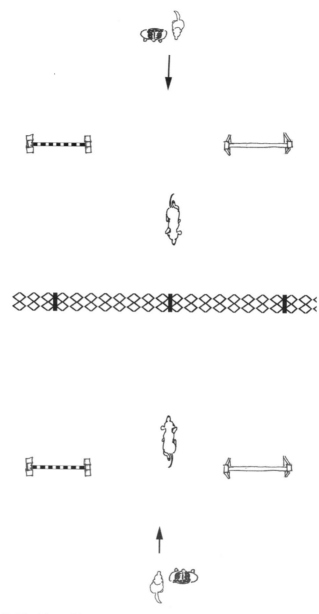

Figure 24.8: Working with a partner, send your dogs towards a central gate at the same time. The slower dog will likely sit when the faster dog's handler commands the sit for her dog.

Directed Jumping

The Exercises ❖ 119

your dog to master the concept without compromising his
go-outs.

👫 Have a helper do something distracting just before or just
after your sit command, such as open or shut a door, toss
a dumbbell, dump a set of articles onto the floor, crinkle a
chip bag, or clang a crate door.

👫 Have a helper standing or sitting on the floor near the
go-out spot, tempting your dog to visit. Refer back to
the *Timing of Proofs* (p. 20) and *Adding a Person Nearby*
(pp. 24-26) sections for ideas. You might start with your
helper outside the ring, and then move her inside the ring.

👤 Put a sticky dot or piece of tape on the floor near the spot
you want your dog to sit at the end of the go-out. He will
be likely to sniff the dot and then forget about the sit.

Proofing Against Stopping Short

Most dogs eventually stop short on a go-out, whether in training or in a trial. While I hope it is in training where you can do
something about it, the chances are good that it will happen in a
trial. To guard against this, be sure to be alert for "cheating." By
cheating, I mean when your dog starts his turn just before your
sit command comes out of your mouth, or even worse, when he
turns to face you and starts to sit before you say anything at all.
If you see this start to happen, I'd recommend that you work on
purposely stopping him short. Most of my beginning students
blanche when I first suggest this, but I think it is an important
step to clarify the meaning of go-out for your dog.

Often, when you first try to stop him short, your dog will
ignore your early sit command and continue on to the spot he
thinks is correct. You may need to keep him on a leash, long-line,
or retractable leash so you can stop him if he ignores your command.

Usually a time or two of asking for a short go-out causes your
dog to stop in that spot the next time. Then you can do whatever
you deem appropriate to show him that this is wrong. As discussed in the *Solutions to Common Go-out Errors* section, I take
my dog by the collar and run him along the ring's centerline all
the way out to the correct spot at the end of the ring. With an experienced dog, I might simply say, "No, GO OUT!"

Directed Jumping

120 ❖ The Art of Proofing

Once my dog can stop anywhere along the go-out path, I re-send him so he turns and continues on his go-out from where he stopped. My goal is to get to the point where I can stop him and resend him multiple times along the go-out path.

Proofing Against Taking a Jump on a Go-out

As I mentioned before, long before I ever did any agility, each of my dogs discovered that jumping a jump on a go-out was a possibility. Along with alternating sending on a go-out and sending over a jump, I test my dog's understanding with the following proofs:

❢ Do a series of go-outs and jumps in one direction, then turn around and do go-outs in the opposite direction. Since your dog has just jumped from that end of the ring, he might jump instead of going out between the jumps correctly.

❢ Do a Retrieve over High Jump first, then move to your go-out launching spot and send on a go-out. If a one-to-one pairing doesn't cause him to jump on a go-out, it might if you do 3–4 jumps first and then a go-out.

People Distractions

A critical exercise to work on before trialing is to have a person in the ring while your dog does go-outs. Have a friend start about 20 feet away, but within the ring boundary, and gradually move closer to the go-out line. Have her start with her back to your dog. When he succeeds, your friend can become more and more distracting. See the section on *Adding a Person Nearby* (pp. 24-26) for more ideas.

Some dogs will go to your friend; some will avoid her. Help or correct as needed. When your dog succeeds with your friend standing or sitting still, have her wander around randomly. This exercise is likely to cause some confusion. Stay cool and help your dog do his go-outs correctly.

Gloves and Go-outs

When I was first showing in Utility in the mid-1980s, the *Moving Stand for Exam* exercise did not exist. Instead, there was a 3–minute group stand for exam—an exercise I wasn't sorry to see go away. This meant the *Directed Retrieve* exercise immediately

Directed Jumping

preceded the *Directed Jumping* exercise. Dogs who retrieved a corner glove would often return to that corner of the ring on their go-outs. They would lose a lot of points for poor go-outs, and would often fail the exercise because they took the jump on the glove corner side twice.

Then the *Moving Stand* was inserted between the *Directed Retrieve* and *Directed Jumping* in Utility. This means that confusion between the glove retrieve and the go-out isn't quite as much of a problem as it used to be. However, because so many dogs still incorrectly go to corners on their go-outs, it's smart to teach your dog the difference between a glove retrieve and a go-out.

Don't start this proofing until your dog understands each exercise separately. Your dog should find it easier to differentiate between gloves and go-outs if your cueing system is clear, whether you use words, hand signals, or some combination of the two, to communicate which exercise you are about to do. My cue for the mark for the glove retrieve is my left hand alongside the right side of my dog's head, all fingers pointing forward (Figure 24.9). During training, if my dog needs a verbal reminder, I add the cue MARK. Before a go-out, I use the index finger of my left hand pointing forward and I say SEE IT? or LOOK (Figure 24.10).

Stage 1—Go-outs with Decoy Glove

At this stage, you are simply doing go-outs with a decoy glove in a corner. Start with one glove in the corner of the ring to your right as you face that end—the number 3 glove—and have your go-out props in place in the center (Figure 24.11). To help your

Figure 24.9: My glove marking cue.

Figure 24.10: My go-out marking cue.

Directed Jumping

122 ❖ The Art of Proofing

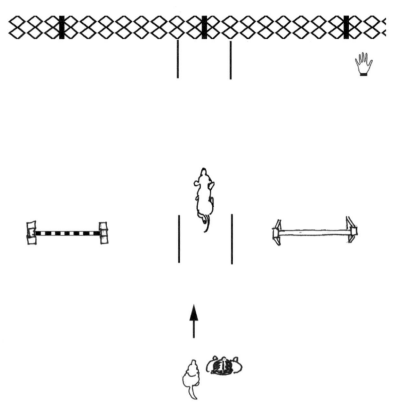

Figure 24.11: Stage 1 of glove go-out proofing, with a glove in the right corner. Start close to the end of the go-out and work your way back to a full-length go-out. The props (sticks shown here) are in place to help ensure a straight go-out.

dog to succeed, set up for the go-out fairly close to the target, perhaps ten to fifteen feet away.

Gradually start the go-out farther from the target until you can do a full-length go-out with a glove in a corner, and over time, move the glove closer to the center, until it is as close as several feet from the target. This may take many training sessions.

Start close to the target again, but with a glove in the left corner—the number 1 glove. Repeat the steps you used when the glove was on your right.

Directed Jumping

The Exercises ❖ 123

Stage 2—Glove Retrieve Followed by Go-out

Next, do repetitions of a glove retrieve followed by a go-out. I recommend that you start with whichever corner glove your dog finds easier, so he can learn the concept more quickly. After he has retrieved the corner glove, send him on a go-out. During this stage, don't replace the glove before you do the go-out.

I find that dogs usually need to repeat either the glove retrieve or the go-out, because this proof tends to expose weaknesses, or at least it shows a preference for one of the exercises. If you have just done a number 3 glove retrieve, and your dog veers towards that corner on his subsequent go-out, repeat the go-out until he does a full-length one correctly. If he veers towards his go-out target during a glove retrieve, repeat the glove retrieve until he does that right. When he can alternate between retrieving a glove from either corner and doing a full-length go-out without errors, go on to the next stage.

Stage 3—Retrieve Followed by Go-out with Glove in Place

After your dog retrieves a corner glove, replace the glove in the corner, but send your dog on a go-out. I start with the right corner glove—number 3—because I can block my dog's view of it somewhat, but do whichever one seems more likely to be successful. Repeat this sequence with that corner until you've had at least three correct pairs of a corner glove followed by a full-length go-out. This may take ten minutes; it might take several days.

Once the first side is mastered, start over again with the glove in the other corner.

Gradually move the glove closer to the go-out spot until it is clearly in his line of vision from the start of the go-out. When he can do this without faltering, scatter more gloves throughout your training area and teach him to ignore them all.

Put other items out as well: a dumbbell, a scent article, a toy, etc. He is supposed to ignore these distractions and think only about the go-out.

Stage 4—Poison Bird

In retriever field training, there is an advanced concept called a *poison bird*. In this, the retriever sees a bird fall, but instead of immediately retrieving that bird, he must instead do a blind retrieve, i.e., must go retrieve a bird he hasn't seen fall. This is done

Directed Jumping

124 ❖ The Art of Proofing

with a combination of "lining," which is essentially what go-outs are, and handling, like what you must do for the directed retrieve in UKC Utility. Once the dog returns with the blind-retrieve bird, he may then get the poison bird. You can apply this concept to your advanced go-out training.

Once your dog is solid on the previous stages and before you start the poison bird concept, try this: stand at your go-out launching pad, toss a dumbbell off to the side, and send your dog to retrieve it. After he returns his dumbbell, send him on a go-out. Often, dogs will veer towards where the dumbbell just landed. This is a good preparation step for what follows.

When I first start the poison bird lesson, I face the corner of the ring to my right, and toss the dumbbell there (Figure 24.12). Then I turn to face the go-out spot, cue my dog as usual, and send him on his go-out. If my dog heads for the dumbbell, I stop him with a verbal correction, bring him back to the centerline, just before where he veered, and cue him and send him again. I might move closer to the target end of the ring. I might need to bring back more go-out props. Once he manages his go-out correctly, he gets to retrieve his dumbbell from the corner. Once my dog successfully sees me throw my dumbbell to the corner and then does a straight go-out before retrieving the dumbbell, I throw the dumbbell in the direction of the jump that is on the right side of the ring. This means my dog will have to run past the tempting dumbbell on his way out. While some dogs do head for the dumbbell, others respond by avoiding it with a big arc or veer in the opposite direction. If need be, use some familiar guides (broad jump boards, sticks on the ground) to help reduce the arc. (Figures 24.3–24.5)

Eventually, I will toss my dumbbell to the far end of the ring. If I can't throw it accurately that far, I'll walk out and place it, then return to my dog and send him on his go-out.

Once one side is going smoothly, I start over with a throw to the closer left corner of the ring. For the toy-crazed dog, I do this proof with a toy once they can do it with a dumbbell. For a food-loving dog, I do it with treats.

Directed Jumping

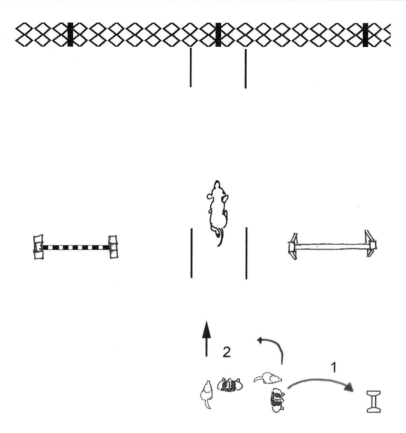

Figure 24.12: Stage 4 of glove go-out proofing: poison bird. Start by facing the right corner of the ring (1) and toss your dumbbell there. Without letting your dog retrieve it, turn to face the far end of the ring (2), cue your go-out and send your dog. The props (sticks shown here) are in place to help ensure a straight go-out.

Utility Jumping

During the Utility Directed Jumping exercise, a judge will be standing at the same end of the ring as you are when you direct your dog to a jump. The judge can stand on the same side as the jump your dog should take, the opposite side, or directly behind you. Acclimate your dog to having someone stand in each of these different places. Your back is frequently to the crowd when doing

126 ❖ The Art of Proofing

Directed Jumping, so your dog needs to be prepared for the normal movement of people and their dogs behind you.

- ♛ Start with a helper a fair distance away from your dog and not looking at him, at your end of the ring. If your dog pays no attention to this person, have her move closer to where you are standing the next time.

- ♛ Put an object, such as a training bag, an extra jump standard, or a chair, several feet to the inside of either jump. Many dogs will go between the object and jump instead of jumping. I stumbled upon this proof when my son Chris was very young. I would train Directed Jumping while he zoomed around the training area in his toddler walker. My Australian Terrier Casey seemed to think that just running around Chris was an adequate response to my jump cues.

> When you are first proofing the jumps, don't combine them with go-outs. Instead, place your dog in the go-out location to simplify and keep your lesson focused on the jumps.

- ♛ Have a friend stand about 3 feet to the inside post of one of the jumps. At first she should have her back to your dog (Figure 24.13). When your dog handles this with ease, your friend should turn around toward the jump or the center of the ring (Figure 24.14). Finally, she should face your dog (Figure 24.15). Many dogs will go between your helper and the jump instead of jumping. If this happens, you may need to simplify and move yourself or your dog closer to the jump.

- ♛ Have your friend tempt your dog with a toy during the previous proof (Figure 24.16).

- ♛ Have your helper gradually move toward your dog until she is finally standing between your dog and the jump that you will signal. This may take a number of training sessions. The only place she shouldn't stand is directly between you and your dog since your helper would then block your signal.

- ♛ Have you friend walk randomly around the ring while you direct your dog to either jump.

Directed Jumping

The Exercises ❖ 127

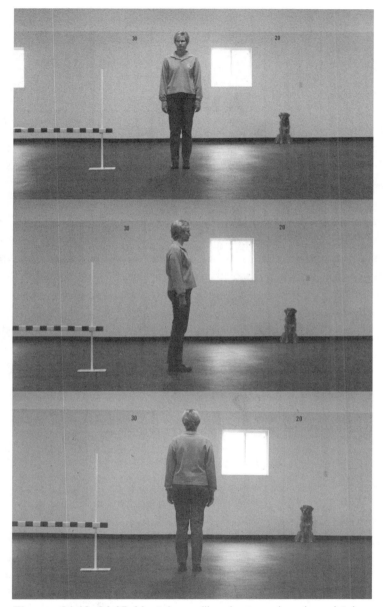

Figures 24.13–24.15: Most dogs will make some jumping mistakes when someone is standing next to the jump they are supposed to take. Often, the dog runs between the person and the jump. Start with your helper standing with her back to your dog, then facing the jump or the center, then facing your dog.

Directed Jumping

128 ❖ The Art of Proofing

Figures 24.16: Gryffin is jumping correctly in spite of the huge temptation Belinda's toy presents him.

- Vary the background your dog sees behind the bar jump, since he may perceive the background as actually being in his landing path.
  - Have him jump fairly close to baby gates or to a wall.
  - Have him jump a high jump positioned near a white wall.
  - Practice with a variety of activities on the other side of the gate, any of which might distract your dog from jumping correctly.
- Have your distracter walk in quickly to check your dog's front after he jumps, which is a common motion for a judge to make. This is an important proof because your dog might go right to heel when a judge walks up quickly behind him.
- Place the jumps farther apart or closer together than the standard 18–20 feet. Positioning them farther apart will make the jumping half of the exercise harder; closer together makes the go-outs harder, because it might tempt your dog to jump on a go-out. If you show in CKC or UKC Utility, the rings are usually narrower than AKC rings, so

this is especially important to work on before showing in either of those venues.

- Hang a coat or floppy hat from the uprights of the jump.

- Drape a toy over the top of a jump.

- Place attractive toys or other objects directly outside ring gates between a jump and the far end of the ring.

- Scatter one to several toys or other objects around the ring. After a successful jump, front, or finish, I sometimes release my toy-crazed dog to retrieve one of these distracting toys.

- Line up chairs and crates beside one side of your ring. Have people sit in the chairs, with a dog or two in crates or at their handler's feet. You can add training bags and coolers to more closely simulate a crowded trial.

- Place your dog in the various places where he might end up if he does a poor go-out (the grey area of Figure 24.17). For example, he might run to a corner. He needs to be able to take the jump on that side as well as the jump that is on the far side of the ring. Proof not only for corner go-outs but also for short, off-to-the-side go-outs.

- When your dog can jump either jump from any location in the ring that would be a qualifying go-out, lean your upper body toward one side of the ring while signaling the jump on the opposite side. When your dog can respond correctly when you lean the wrong way, you can take a step or two to one side and then signal the opposite jump.

- I normally use both a verbal and hand signal to direct my dog to a jump, but with a dog who is making wrong choices frequently, a signal alone can improve this, since he must look at you to see your cue. My Australian Terrier Rio would head to a jump when the judge would command "high jump" or "bar jump." When I stopped using a verbal command with him, it did improve his passing ratio.

Directed Jumping

130 ❖ The Art of Proofing

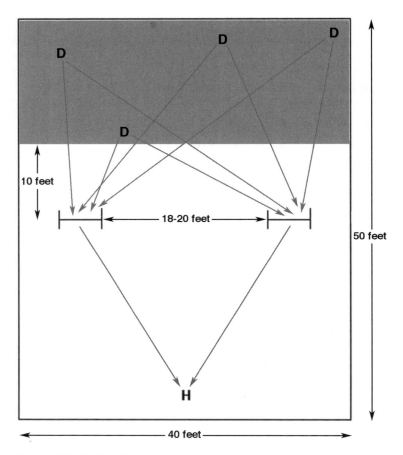

Figure 24.17: The D's show some of the critical positions from which your dog should be able to successfully jump.

Directed Jumping

The End?

I personally love innovation. It prevents boredom for my dogs and me. This keeps me thinking up new twists on old proofs. When I was writing this book, I kept thinking I would never finish, because I kept thinking of new proofs to add. But there does come a time to say "Enough!" I hope that these ideas have fueled your imagination, and that you have come up with many new proofing techniques, or variations on a theme, that you have tried out with your dog.

Don't rush. Let your dog learn how to cope with proofing and distractions over time, with gradual exposure and patience. Training and proofing your dog can and should be an enjoyable process for you both. I hope you can make it so, and that the proofing you do better prepares you for your obedience title quest.

Are you ready? Go proof!

Appendix A:
Truth is Stranger than Fiction

Now and then, when I see a novel problem crop up at a trial, I file it away in my mind as something new to proof against. During a trial in which a Golden Retriever found a very creative way to NQ in Utility A, I started asking other exhibitors this question "What is the weirdest thing you've seen or had happen to you when at an obedience trial?" My thanks go to the many friends who responded. I got several interesting and funny responses. Here is the one I saw that spawned my question:

The Open handler in the ring to the left of the Utility A ring threw her dumbbell for the Retrieve on Flat. It bounced up against the gate on the right side of the ring about three quarters of the length of the ring away from the handler. The judge decided to fetch the dumbbell himself. I'm still not sure why, since the dumbbell was still in the ring. As the judge started to walk out to retrieve the dumbbell, the Golden retriever in the Utility A ring to the right was doing a go-out, saw the dumbbell land, made a 90^0 left turn, went to the gate, reached under and retrieved the dumbbell. The dog then returned over the Utility high jump to her handler. The Utility judge did not rejudge the go-out.

When one exhibitor's dog kicked her dumbbell out of the ring into a center aisle, the dog hopped over the gating to get it. Instead of jumping back over the gating, she wove her way through the crowd, into the ring behind her handler, and around to give her a perfect front.

A trial was in a covered building that was fully open on one side. The excess matting was in rolls about a yard behind where the dogs were lined up for their Open group stays. A crazy, kamikaze squirrel was running back and forth behind the dogs on top of the rolls of excess matting. None of the dogs blinked, but the handlers, who could see what was going on from their hiding spot, were pretty anxious!

An absent-minded judge examined dogs during Signals. The same judge also tried to repeat the Drop on Recall, having forgotten the team he was judging had already done it.

At an outdoor fall trial, the ring was next to a turkey farm. They were butchering turkeys and there was an awful lot of gobbling and scared turkey noises as they caught them.

After a dog would sit on the go-out, a certain judge would cross behind the handler, and then give the opposite jump from where he was now standing. Many green dogs take the wrong jump when someone does this.

An absent minded judge took the Utility A dog's article from the handler, went to the pile, stood there, and then finally said "Send your dog!" without ever putting the article in the pile. The handler sent her dog, who looked and looked and looked. The dog finally just stood there and the handler happened to see that the judge was still holding the article.

One judge stood near the middle of the Drop on Recall and gave the signal to drop the dog right across from him.

* * * * *

Many fairground facilities have low flying birds. They might even land in a ring and hop around, hunting for food.

Many fairgrounds have livestock manure in the ring.

At an outdoor show, you might have a small plane circle overhead or even land nearby.

Sometimes, a bump into a baby gate knocks over the whole section of ring gating.

Rude conformation handlers sometimes let their dog pee on the ring gating behind dogs on stays. With really bad luck, the peeing dog might hit one of the staying dogs.

Proof for food such as hotdogs, hamburgers, and popcorn coming into the ring.

Be prepared for the impatient judge who holds out his clipboard for your scented article as soon as you pick it up to scent it.

Make sure your dog will continue to sit stay when the judge raises their arm to signal the steward to have the handlers return from out of sight stays. Some dogs will go down on the sit when they see this signal.

Appendix A: Truth is Stranger than Fiction

134 ❖ The Art of Proofing

Expose your dog to dogs whose breathing is labored, such as a bulldog.

Make sure your dog isn't upset if a judge sneezes, sniffs, or burps while doing the exam on the stand exercises in Novice or Utility.

Make sure that your dog can cope with all of the handlers returning early on a stay and then leaving again with the dogs in the original position, especially filing in and out of the ring for the Open out-of-sight stays.

Make sure your dog can stay put with someone stumbling and even falling down in the ring nearby.

What would your dog do if another dog was just beyond the gating, trying to retrieve your dog's dumbbell?

What would your dog do if a dog from the next ring sailed over the barrier and started zooming around your ring? What would *you* do?

* * * * *

While you can never prepare for everything, thorough proofing increases your chances of success.

Appendix A: Truth is Stranger than Fiction

Appendix B: About the Author

I have lived in the Ann Arbor area almost my whole life. As a teen, I was in a local 4-H horse club and rode and showed horses. This formed the basis for my love of working with animals. The owner of the farm where I rode, Sheila Dunn, also bred and showed Welsh Corgis and Australian Terriers. When my husband Fritz and I got married in 1984, Sheila gave us an IOU for a Corgi puppy for a wedding present. Another friend gave us a crate for our future puppy, a gift that I still use to this day.

By early 1985, my desire for a puppy had reached fever pitch, but with no Corgi puppies on Sheila's horizon, we got our first Australian Terrier, Casey, from her instead. My goal: to earn a UD (Utility Dog) title with her. I had no idea what that actually meant, nor what hard work it would entail.

A year after getting Casey, Helen Szostak loaned us Tramp, a 9-month-old Flat-Coated Retriever, to see if I was allergic to the breed—Tramp stayed, since I wasn't—and by then, I was hooked on dog sports. While training them for obedience, I showed Casey and Tramp in conformation, the former unsuccessfully, the latter to my first breed championship. I started teaching competition obedience at the Ann Arbor Dog Training Club in the mid-1980's, thanks to Gail Dapogny's strong encouragement, and found it much more enjoyable than my computer programming day job.

When our son Chris was born in 1989, I didn't want to put him in daycare to return to the corporate job full time. My dream of starting a dog training business came to life in 1990, thanks to Fritz's willingness to let me try my hand at entrepreneurship. It allowed me to be a stay-at-home mom by day and teach classes a couple of evenings a week in a cold and cluttered 2.5 car garage that I rented.

In 1992, when I was pregnant with our second son, Ryan, we moved to a smaller property, with a nicer house, a better location, and a pole barn bigger than the rented garage. We added on to the pole barn, finishing the insides, and my business continued to grow. From these humble beginnings has grown the flourishing Northfield Dog Training.

In 1995, Judy Byron and I formed a joint venture to write a book and produce a training video. Our video, *Positively Fetching: Teaching the Obedience Retrieves Using Food*, came out in 1995, and in 1998, we self-published *Competition Obedience: A Balancing Act*. Both of them have continued to be popular training aids for people all around the country and even internationally.

Sadly, Judy passed away from ovarian cancer in 2000. I have always been grateful that she was able to enjoy the success of our publications before her death. They are her legacy to the obedience world.

When I added agility classes in the late 1990's, my business started bursting at the seams of our original building. This prompted me to start the construction process to build a much larger building, again with the gracious support of my husband. My business now resides in what my family sometimes refers to as Adele's Airplane Hanger in our country backyard. While I personally focus on competition obedience and Rally classes, I have a wonderful staff of women, all dog trainers first, and we offer all levels of obedience and agility classes and lessons.

Most of the material for this book has been gathered during my weekly obedience proofing classes, in private lessons, and in the training and trialing of my own dogs. There's nothing like being in the trenches of competition to make you aware of holes in your training program. I love to invent some new twist on an old proofing or teaching technique to better explain to the dogs what we want them to do for us.

While obedience continues to be my core training activity, I have also done tracking, agility, and conformation. Since Gryffin came into my life, I have embarked into serious field training with my Flat-Coats. I am fascinated by how much obedience and field training overlap, and am really enjoying learning a new sport.

In late 2004, I applied for Provisional status as a Rally judge, and in early 2005, took the plunge and applied to judge Novice obedience.

When I'm not taking care of my dogs or my business, I'm busy with my family, reading, exercising, singing with a local women's chorus, or working in my organic vegetable garden.

Appendix B: About the Author

Appendix C: My Dogs & Their Titles

Casey (U–CD Hott Pursuitt on the Farm Am/Can UD) 1984–1997: Casey was my first dog and my first Australian Terrier. She was bold and sassy at times, scared and timid at others. She taught me persistence, since it took 21 trials to earn all 3 legs for her UD. She earned my first all-breed High in Trial at a Canadian trial, tying with Tramp in a huge Novice B class with a 199.5 score, absolutely the most brilliant performance of her obedience career. She also came out of three years of retirement to earn HIT at the 1993 Australian Terrier National Specialty, the first to offer obedience, beating out her house mate Rio.

Tramp (Am/Can Ch. OTCh. U–CD Grousemoor Some Like It Hot TD WC; Can UD) 1985–1994: Tramp was my first breed champion, my first OTCh., my first TD, my first WC. She was a grand introduction to the wonderful world of Flat-Coated Retrievers, and I'll always be grateful to Helen Szostak for letting me steal Tramp away from her when Tramp was 9 months old. Tramp had a litter of puppies for Helen. She and I were pregnant at the same time, and she certified for her TD during that time, and passed the tracking test at the National when I was 8 months pregnant. She earned my first AKC HIT out of Open B and was a particularly fine Utility dog. She had several tournament placements and numerous HITs and HCs, including one earned one week before my younger son was born.

Rio (Ch. OTCh. U–CD Free For All on the Farm UDX TD; Can CDX) 1988–1996: Rio was my soul mate. He was the first Australian Terrier to earn the OTCh. title, and my first UDX. He was a funny, sunny, happy little dog who did just about everything I asked of him with joy and reckless abandon. He had tournament placements at the Open level and numerous HITs and HCs while earning his OTCh. and UDX. I was still competing with him when kidney failure stole him from me at the young age of 8. His loss hit me extremely hard because we were so close.

Treasure (Ch. OTCh. U–UD Grousemoor Forget Me Not UDX RN OA OAJ WC; Can UD; RL2) 1993–2006: Treasure burst into my life at a crazy time. My sons were 1 and 4 years old, I had three older dogs, and I had a growing business. In looking back, I cannot imagine life without her. Many people have told me that they base their image of perfect heeling on what they saw when they watched Treasure and me heeling together. She earned nu-

138 ❖ The Art of Proofing

merous tournament placements, including 1st place in the Pup-aroni Central Regional Novice division in Detroit in 1996. She also had many HITs and HCs in her career. She earned her one and only Junior Hunter leg at 11.5 years of age. At 12 years of age, she could still heel accurately, and better than two-year old in-training Gryffin.

Java (OTCh. U–CDX Riversides Magen's Starbucks UDX2 RE AX AXJ; Can CD; RL3) 1997– 2011: Java was my first Border Terrier and he was wickedly smart as so many of his breed are. He frequently tested whether or not a command meant the same thing today as it did yesterday. He placed 3rd in the Novice divisions at the 1999 Classic and 2000 World Series tournaments. When he finished his OTCh. in 2004, he was the first Border Terrier in ten years to do so. I kept finding myself needing to frequently change what I did when I trained and trialed him, making for an interesting challenge. He forced me to learn several things I wish I hadn't had to learn, but I think I'm a better trainer from having had him in my life.

Joker (Kandu's The Joker Is Wild UD RE; RL2) 2001– : We bought Border Terrier Joker for my son Chris when Chris was 12. Chris trained him in several obedience and agility classes, but had little interest in competing with him. Joker had a strong desire to work, so after Chris left for college, I gradually trained him and put titles on him. High accuracy was not his strong point, but we enjoyed the journey, he taught me useful stuff, and he earned his RE and UD when he was 10.

Gryffin (Ch. OTCh. Grousemoor Gryffindor UDX OM1 RE MH WCX; RL2) 2003– 2012: Working with Flat-Coated Retriever Gryffin was usually a roller coaster ride. He was the highest drive dog I'd ever worked with, and a physical outlet for that energy was crucial. He dragged me into the fascinating world of hunt tests and retriever training as a way to expend some of that boundless energy. He had a lot of talent for it, and he taught me to love the hunt test game. He was the first dog I've started by showing in Rally obedience, and I found it to be a fine way to introduce a new dog to the ring without the stringent requirements of the obedience ring. In 2010, he finished his OTCh. title (my 5th) in January and his MH in August, a completely magical experience.

Ty (Ch. Grousemoor Timeless UDX OM2 RE; RL1) 2004– : Ty and her sister Vega stayed with my family for a week or so when they were four months old. After Treasure's death, Ty joined our

Appendix C: My Dogs & Their Titles

family when she was 16 months old, and quickly became my little shadow. She went on to earn many titles during our years together, and 20-some OTCh. points and a couple of HITs, but she and I struggled in our relationship quite a bit. After a great deal of soul searching, in April 2013 we placed her in a new home where she is a single dog, and she brings a lot of joy to her new owner.

Sonic (Coastalight Primetime CD BN GN RE SH WCX) 2011-
: when Flat-Coated Retriever Sonic flew home with me from her Vancouver Island birthplace, my life was very different than it had been when puppy Gryffin had come home. With my sons no longer needing Mom Chaffeur, I had quite a bit more time to train her. I started making short training videos on her early training, posting them on my YouTube channel. Search for 'Adele Yunck' or 'Sonic the FCR' on YouTube and you'll find a large assortment of videos. She is just getting started in Novice B as I write this, having earned her SH when she was just over 2, and her GN title the following fall. I did that first as I wanted ring experience for her, but wanted time to polish her heeling, as well as firm up her Stand for Exam and Sit Stay, which can be problematic for young and social Flat-Coats. She has a ton of energy and loves to work with me. I look forward to working toward her advanced obedience and field titles in the years to come.

??? 2014-: I hope to have a new Border Terrier puppy sometime later this spring. I'd like a new little one while Joker is still around to help raise it, since he is so good at that job.

Appendix C: My Dogs & Their Titles

Glossary

AKC (American Kennel Club) (www.akc.org): the national dog registration service that promotes the sport of purebred dogs. They are the sanctioning body for dog shows and trials of many types, including obedience and Rally trials.

Anticipation: when your dog does an exercise or part of an exercise without waiting for your cue (verbal command or hand signal). Sometimes, this means an NQ, sometimes just points off.

Automatic correction: this means adding a physical correction after a command automatically. I don't want to use one every time I give a cue, but will use one frequently if my dog is being lazy about responding promptly to a given command.

Automatic finish: when your dog does a finish without any cue or signal from you, i.e., he anticipates the finish.

CKC (Canadian Kennel Club) (www.ckc.ca): the Canadian counterpart to the AKC.

CD (Companion Dog) title: must earn three qualifying scores in the Novice obedience class.

CDX (Companion Dog Excellent) title: must earn three qualifying scores in the Open obedience class.

CR: refers to a *conditioned reinforcer*. Your CR is your way of marking what you like about what your dog has just done. It can be a click with a clicker, a special word or sound, or even a flash of light. It precedes a treat. When I say "CR" in the text, I mean "use your CR and give your dog a treat."

Disqualified: a dog who is blind or deaf; has been changed in appearance for cosmetic reasons other than what is deemed acceptable in a breed's standard; or has attacked or attempted to attack a person in the ring. This is a serious event, unlike an NQ, which happens to everyone sooner or later!

Distracter: refers to another person who is helping you to proof your dog.

Distraction: anything that catches your dog's attention, causing him to lose focus on the task at hand. It usually refers to something inanimate, often an object your dog finds attractive—a squeaky toy or a tempting treat. It might also be a noise or smell of some kind or people or another animal.

Drop your dog: this means to have your dog perform a down.

Excused: the judge will excuse you from the remaining exercises if your dog is lame; if he attacks another dog in the ring or appears dangerous to other dogs in the ring; is taped, stitched or bandaged in anyway; if he is out of control; if you discipline your dog in the ring (note that an extra command or two does not constitute discipline).

Habituated: comfortable in the current environment.

Habituation: the time it takes your dog to get comfortable in a new environment.

HC (High Combined): an award given at obedience trials to the dog with the highest total combined score from the Open B and Utility classes.

HIT (High in trial): an award given at obedience trials to the dog with the highest score of the day from the regular classes.

Leg, earn a leg: when a dog earns a qualifying score towards a title, it is called "earning a leg." For the CD, CDX, and UD titles, dogs must earn three legs to complete a title at that level. This is also true when earning Rally titles. See also *qualifying score.*

Negative reinforcer: precedes a response, such as a jerk on a leash that causes a dog to come. The negative stimulus *stops* (you remove the unpleasant stimulus) when the dog responds correctly.

NQ: non-qualify. Your dog fails to perform one or more exercises according to the regulations. See *qualifying score* for further explanation.

OTCh. (Obedience Trial Champion title): to earn this title, your dog must have earned at least 100 points; a first place in Open B; a first place in Utility B; and an additional first place in either class. It is the only competitive obedience title, in that you must beat other teams in order to earn it. The number of points earned in a given class depend on the number of dogs competing. Points are earned by placing in Open B or Utility B.

Phantom Food: your distracter holds her empty hand like she is holding a treat out to your dog, usually with her fingers and thumb close together.

Glossary

142 ❖ The Art of Proofing

Pile: common name for the placement of the scent articles in Utility. The articles are supposed to be placed 6" apart. They are not piled on top of each other.

Positive reinforcer: you add something desirable immediately *after* a response, such as giving your dog a treat as soon as he comes to you. See also *reinforcer*.

Punisher: a stimulus that *decreases* a behavior. A *positive punisher* means you add something unpleasant during a behavior with the goal that the behavior decreases. A *negative punisher* means you remove something desirable to decrease a behavior.

Qualifying score: in AKC obedience, this means that a dog and handler have earned more than 50% of the points for each exercise with a total score of at least 170 points. In AKC Rally, a dog and handler must earn at least 70 points out of 100 to qualify.

Rally: a relatively new sport, Rally is a hybrid of obedience and agility, combining the open communication of agility—you are allowed to talk as much as you want—and sequential courses with obedience-related exercises. It is a fine stepping-stone to the obedience ring.

Reinforcer: any stimulus that causes a behavior to happen more frequently. See also *positive reinforcer* and *negative reinforcer*.

Ring: a rectangular area in which you compete at an obedience trial. There are barriers of some type used to define the sides, unless the room is the same size as the ring. In my area of the country (the Midwest), rings are most often defined with baby gates and stanchions to hold them up.

Tab: a very short (6–10") leash used during the transition from on-leash to off-leash.

Target: typically a round plastic lid, such as a yogurt lid. By teaching your dog that it is valuable to go to a target, you simplify teaching several exercises, especially Utility go-outs.

UKC (United Kennel Club) (www.ukcdogs.com): a national dog registry that sanctions many types of dog sports, and allows spayed and neutered mixed breed dogs to compete for performance titles.

UD (Utility Dog) title: must earn three qualifying scores in the Utility class.

UDX (Utility Dog Excellent) title: must earn qualifying scores in both Open B and Utility B at ten separate trials. Dog must have his UD before starting to accumulate UDX legs.

Glossary

Visit our web site at www.northfielddogtraining.com to order any of Adele's books and DVDs.

Totally Fetching

Teaching and Proofing the Obedience Retrieves

a DVD and booklet by

Adele Yunck and Judy Byron

This 70–minute video:

- Teaches you how to use a conditioned reinforcer.

- Shows many dogs and handlers learning to retrieve.

- The 48–page booklet provides an easy reference to the information in the video.

- Includes in-depth examples at each stage of the retrieve process as well as problem solving.

- Brings the chapter on proofing the retrieve from this book to the screen.

Competition Obedience:
A Balancing Act

This nearly 400–page book covers all of AKC obedience, from picking a puppy through earning titles at the Novice, Open, and Utility level. It covers how to train with a conditioned reinforcer and how to use corrections fairly. The authors explain not only how to teach an exercise, but how to proof it. It is extensively illustrated and has a comprehensive index.

Notes

Notes

Index

A

Adjacent activity 14
Agility 14
Anticipation 21, 140
  Recall 62
Applause 11, 33
Attention 22–34
  Corrections 23
  Distance 23
  Front 22
  Group proofing 31–35
  Heel position 22
  Proofing 22–34
  Solo proofing 29–30
Attention loss 23
Automatic correction 7, 140
Automatic finish 54, 140

B

Baby gate 30, 56, 57, 69, 72, 74, 75,
    96, 113, 133
Ball 29, 30, 117
Balloons 26, 30
Broad Jump 23, 82–84
Broad jump boards as a chute 109,
    110, 124

C

Call to heel
  Moving Stand 68
CD (Companion Dog) title 140
CDX (Companion Dog Excellent) title
    140
CKC (Canadian Kennel Club) 140
Clicker 5
Clothing
  Signals 15, 85, 86, 90
Collar 7

Competition Obedience: A Balancing
    Act 2, 5, 22, 145
Conformation ring 14
Correction
  Automatic 7
  For loss of attention 23
  Go-outs 114
  Physical 6, 23
  Retrieve 69
  Stays 45–46
  Theory 7
  Types of 7–8
  Verbal 6
CR (Conditioned Reinforcer) 5, 140
Creeping 24, 88, 92, 116, 117

D

Directed Jumping 19, 23, 54, 56,
    108–129
  Go-outs 109–124
  Jumping 125–129
Directed Retrieve 100–107
Disqualified 140
Distance 19
Distance Attention 23
Distracter 5, 140
Distraction 5, 140
Don't Shoot the Dog 3
Doors, slamming 12, 14
Dots, sticky 16, 30, 69, 82, 110, 119
Down stay 45–52
Drop on Recall 19, 24, 54, 59–64
Drop your dog 141
Dumbbell
  Proofing of 69–77
  Proofing with 12, 20, 62–63
  Retrieve over the High Jump 78–81

148 ❖ The Art of Proofing

E

Empty the toy box 31–32
Environment 10, 141
  Adjacent activity 14
  Baby gate 30, 56, 57, 69, 72, 74, 75, 96, 113, 133
  Flooring 12
  Footing 12
  Habituated 3, 28, 141
  Habituation 141
  Noises and Noise Level 11–13
  People 10
  Smells 14–15
  Time of day 13
  Weather 13–14
Equipment
  Baby gate 30, 56, 57, 69, 72, 74, 75, 96, 113, 133
  Collar 7
  Pinch collar 7
  Tab 142
  Target 54, 55, 92, 109, 110, 113, 114, 117, 122, 123, 124, 142
Escape and avoidance training 7
Exam 66
  Novice 66
  Utility 66
Excused 141

F

Figure 8 40, 40–44
Finishes 56–58
  Automatic 54, 140
Flies 15
Flooring 12
Food 14, 15, 25
Food-toss sit 24, 116
Food vendors 14
Footing 12
Front attention 22, 28
Fronts 53–55

G

Gloves 100–107
  Mark 101, 102, 106
  Mark cue 121
Gloves and Go-outs 120–125
  Poison bird 123
Go-out
  Mark 115
  Mark cue 121
Go-outs 109–124
  Corrections 114
  Props 109, 114
Go-out sit
  People distractions 120
Group attention proofing 31–35

H

Habituated 3, 28, 141
Habituation 141
Hair balls 16
HC (High Combined) 141
Heeling 36–39
  Into Moving Stand 65
Heel position attention 22, 28
HIT (High in trial) 141

J

Judge's cues 21
  Finishes 58
  Recalls 59
  Signal Exercise 86

K

Karen Pryor
  Don't Shoot the Dog 3

L

Leg 141

M

Mark
  Glove cue 121
  Gloves 101, 102
  Gloves cue 121
  Go-out 115
  Go-out cue 121
Mark a behavior with CR 5, 6, 140
Mark an error with verbal correction
    45, 47, 53, 58, 59, 69, 114
Mice 14
Mistakes, being prepared for them
    9–10
Moving distracter 32–33
Moving Stand 21, 24, 65, 67, 68, 91,
    120, 121
  Call to heel 68
  Finish 68
  Heeling 65

N

Negative reinforcement 7
Negative reinforcer 8, 141
Noises 34
Noises and noise level 11–13
Novice
  Figure 8 40–44
  Finishes 56–58
  Fronts 53–55
  Heeling 36–39
  Recall 59–61
  Stand for Exam 66–69
  Stays 45–52
NQ 21, 99, 109, 132, 140, 141

O

Odors. *See* Smells
Open
  Broad Jump 82–84
  Drop on Recall 59–64
  Figure 8 40–44

Heeling 36–39
Retrieve on Flat 69–77
Retrieve over High Jump 78–81
Stays 45–52
OTCh 141

P

People 10
People distractions 24
  On go-out sit 120
Petting 26. *See also* Exam
Phantom Food 5, 25, 41, 49, 61, 70,
    88, 141
Physical corrections 6, 23
Pinch collar 7
Poison bird
  Gloves and Go-Outs 123–125
Positive reinforcement 6
Positive reinforcer 142
Progression of proofs 18–19
Proofing
  Against stopping short on go-out
    119
  Broad jump 82–84
  Directed Jumping 108, 125–129
  Directed Retrieve 100–107
  Down stay 45–51
  Drop on Recall 59–64
  Figure 8 40
  Finishes 56–58
  Fronts 53–55
  Gloves 100–107
  Gloves and Go-Outs 120–124
    Poison bird 123
  Go-outs 109–124
  Heeling 36–39
  Moving Stand 65–68
  Recalls 59–64
  Retrieve on Flat 69–77
  Retrieve over High Jump 78–81
  Scent Discrimination 95–99
  Signal Exercise 85–94

Sit on go-out 117–119
Sit stay 45–51
Stand for exam 65–68
Stand stay 65
Proofs, timing of 20
Pryor, Karen 3
Punisher 142

Q

Qualifying score 142

R

Rally 11, 14, 16, 42, 136, 138, 140
Recalls 24
  Novice 59–64
  Open 59–64
  UKC Drop on Recall 63–64
Reinforcement, negative 7
Reinforcer 142
Retrieve corrections 69
Retrieve on Flat 69–77
Retrieve over High Jump 78–81
Ring 142
Ring enclosures 16
  Baby gates 16
  Curtains 16
  Posts and chains 16

S

Scent Discrimination 95–99
Signal Exercise 23, 24, 52, 85,
    85–94
  Clothes to wear 15, 85, 86, 90
Sit and Down Stays 45–51
Sit on go-out 117–119
Sit stay 45–51
Slamming doors 12, 14
Smells 14–15
Socialization 3
Solo proofing of attention 29–30
Solutions to go-out errors 114–116
  Poor sit on go-out 116

Stopping short 114
Taking a jump on a go-out 114–115
Veering off centerline 114
Staircase
  Progression of proofs 18–19
Stand for Exam 24, 65–68, 120
Stays 45–52
Sticky dots. *See* Dots, sticky
Stopping short on go-out
  Proofing against 119
Stopwatch 26, 51
Sunlight 16, 102–103

T

Tab 66, 142
Target 54, 55, 92, 109, 110, 113,
    114, 117, 122, 123, 124, 142
Temperament 3, 7
Temperature 13
Thunderstorm 13
Time of day 13
Timing of proofs 20
Toy 26, 29, 30, 31, 32, 41, 42,
    45–52, 49, 54, 61, 62, 65–68,
    69, 70, 72, 82, 83, 88, 90, 91,
    98, 99, 117, 120, 123, 124,
    129, 140
  Proofing with 20
Toys 15
Types of corrections 7

U

UD (Utility Dog) 142
UDX (Utility Dog Excellent) 143
UKC Drop on Recall
  Proofing 63–64
UKC (United Kennel Club) 142
Utility
  Directed Jumping 108–129
  Directed Retrieve 100–107
  Gloves 100–107
  Go-outs 109–124

Jumping 125–129
Moving Stand 65–68
Scent Discrimination 95–99
Signal Exercise 85–94

V

Verbal correction 6, 21, 32, 45, 47,
48, 53, 59, 69, 114, 124

W

Weather 13–14
Wind 15